יהוה

# What's In a Name?
## Everlasting Life, Light, and Love

*I will proclaim the name of Yahweh.*
*Give our Elohim (God) the greatness he deserves!*

Deuteronomy 32:3 (NOG)

## Katherine Palmer

## Palmer Enterprises
*Reflecting the Light of God's Word*

**What's In a Name?**
Everlasting Life, Light, and Love
ISBN 978-0-9913483-4-3
Copyright © 2015 by Katherine Palmer
Published by: Palmer Enterprises
1971 Ellsworth Drive
Lakeside Marblehead, OH 43440 USA
Email: palmer2916@roadrunner.com

Front and back cover photos used by permission, courtesy of Cathy Hartman, photographer and author of *Glorious Creation: A Daily Devotional Depicting God's Presence in Nature through Photography*, which is available at www.Amazon.com and www.HisGloriousCreation.com.

Scriptures marked KJV taken from the *King James Version* of the Bible. Free online version at www.BibleGateway.com.

Scripture quotations marked NOG are taken from *The Names of God Bible* and used by permission of Baker Publishing Group. Free online version available at www.BibleGateway.com.

Scripture quotations marked RSB are taken from *The Restoration Study Bible* and used by permission of Yahweh's Restoration Ministry. Free online version available at www.RestorationStudyBible.org.

Scripture quotations marked ISR are taken from *The Scriptures*, copyright by Institute for Scripture Research, used by permission. Free online version available at www.Eliyah.com/TheScriptures.

Scripture verses marked AENT are taken from the *Aramaic English New Testament*. Copyright 2008. Used by permission of Netzari Press.

# What's In a Name?
## Table of Contents

# Acknowledgements

I would like to acknowledge the tremendous help of my dear friend, Cathy Hartman. Her keen insight and editorial assistance was invaluable in undertaking such a weighty subject. Cathy always offered wise, godly counsel, and I could trust her to be honest with me and let me know what made sense and what didn't. Thank you, Cathy, for tackling such a huge project with me. Words cannot express how much I appreciate the many hours you spent editing the book.

I would also like to thank a very close friend, Shirley Mays, who also read through the book and offered very valuable suggestions. When within myself, I doubted that I could pull it all together, she inspired me and gave me gentle reminders to finish the book. Even though I didn't voice my doubt to her, Shirley's strong gift of discernment could sense my floundering, and she always stepped in with encouragement to push me forward to complete the project.

Above all, I thank Yahweh my God and Yahshua (Jesus) my Lord. Only by the power of the Spirit of God was this book able to be birthed and completed. I don't know why He chose me to deliver this message, but I am so very grateful and humbled beyond words. I pray that the message He delivered to me to share with you will accomplish the purpose for which He has called it into being. As Yahweh declares:

*My word, which comes from my mouth, is like the rain and snow. It will not come back to me without results. It will accomplish whatever I want and achieve whatever I send it to do. (Isaiah 55:11 NOG)*

# Introduction

What I'm about to share with you has radically changed my life, and I hope it will change yours, as well. With the chaos, turmoil, and anguish we sometimes experience in our lives and that, indeed, the world is experiencing, right now, we need strength and power to overcome adversity by connecting to a Power greater than ourselves.

Where can we turn in times of pain, confusion, or distress? What should we do when trouble comes knocking at our door? The answer is actually quite simple: call on the name of the LORD.

You may be thinking, "That sounds too easy; there must be a catch." No, it's just that simple. By calling on the name of the LORD, you invite God to intervene on your behalf, and He will then bring you comfort, encouragement, direction, strength, and breakthrough!

Just how important is the name of the LORD? When God was about to send Moses on the most important journey of his life, He revealed the name Yahweh (pronounced *yaw-way)*, meaning, "He is now and forever will be who He is and will be." As you read on, it will become apparent why this straightforward statement is so profound and life-changing.

In revealing His very personal name to Moses, God publicized how He wants to be known for eternity and how He wants us to see Him. The very expression of the LORD's name discloses that He is self-existent, eternal, inexhaustible, and faithful. By calling upon the name of Yahweh, we set in motion His dominion and power in our lives, and a strong love relationship is fostered between the Creator and His beloved creation: YOU!

I pray that what I'm about to unveil regarding God's name will saturate your life with a richness of His presence you may not have experienced before and show you what it really means to call on His magnificent name. Whenever spoken, the name of the LORD becomes a refuge, a strong fortress of safety and protection for His people.

*The Name of* יהוה *(Yahweh) is a strong tower: the righteous run into it and are safe. (Proverbs 18:10 ISR)*

God desires that we draw near to Him; and as we call on His marvelous name in love, reverence, and in an attitude of worship, He will draw near to us. I invite you to experience a richer, deeper, more intimate relationship with the LORD by calling on His most holy name, Yahweh. Get ready to enjoy a more robust connection with the Creator of the universe and Savior of the world, as we explore the burning question:

## "What's in a name?"

יהוה
נֶבָגָ

# Chapter 1
# Distinction

## THE IMPACT OF A NAME

Before we dive into the topic of this book, I'd like to establish the definition of the word *name*. A name is a word or group of words by which a person, animal, place, or thing is known. In addition, a name can refer to authority, such as, "In the name of..."

There are two types of names: common and proper. A common name is general in nature and describes a nonspecific person, animal, place, or thing. It is a designation or title that describes such things as identity, role, function, purpose, reputation, character, authority, or assignment.

A proper name, however, focuses on a distinct and specific person, animal, place, or thing. For example, the term "building" is a common, generic name, while Empire State Building is the proper name of a specific building. Another example: I live in a small town, which is a generic description of where I live, but Lakeside Marblehead is the proper name of the specific town I live in.

This may seem painfully elementary, but I want to make the point that without names, we would have no way to distinguish one person, animal, place, or thing from another, and there would be utter chaos and confusion. Scripture tells us, however, that God is not the author of confusion.

**God is not the author of confusion.**

*For God is not the author of confusion…*
*(1 Corinthians 14:33a KJV)*

*God is not a God of disorder but a God of peace.*
*(1 Corinthians 14:33a NOG)*

Names are so important to God that He instructed Adam to give names to all the animals on earth.

*And out of the ground the LORD God formed every beast of the field, and every fowl of the air; and brought them unto Adam to see what he would call them: and whatsoever Adam called every living creature, that was the name thereof. (Genesis 2:19 KJV)*

If animals' names are important to God, then we must conclude that His name is even more important. In the ancient Hebrew language, names made a statement about a person's character or their purpose. Scripture indicates that names were so significant to God that there were a few times, if the person's given name did not line up with their character or purpose, God renamed them. For example, Yahweh changed Abram's name to Abraham to reflect His promise that Abraham would become the father of many.

*"My promise is still with you. You will become the father of many nations. So your name will no longer be Abram [Exalted Father], but Abraham [Father of Many] because I have made you a father of many nations." (Genesis 17:4-5 NOG)*

To reveal the destiny of His chosen people, Yahweh changed the name of Abraham's grandson, Jacob (heel-catcher, supplanter), to Israel (to strive with God, to overcome with God, then to rule with God).

*And he said, Thy name shall be called no more Jacob, but Israel: for as a prince hast thou power with Elohim and with men, and hast prevailed. (Genesis 32:28 RSB)*

So, we can see that names are very important to God, even to the point where names give us clues about the people we read about in God's Word, the Bible.

One stunning example of the significance of Hebrew names is demonstrated on the next page. The following list of the twelve tribes of Israel displays their names and definitions, and it's interesting to note that the names are given in the exact order of their appearance in Genesis 35:23-26.

| Name | Definition |
|------|-----------|
| **Reuben** | *Behold a son* |
| **Simeon** | *Hearing* |
| **Levi** | *Attached* |
| **Judah** | *Celebrated* |
| **Issachar** | *He will bring a reward* |
| **Zebulun** | *Habitation* |
| **Joseph** | *A tender branch* |
| **Benjamin** | *Son of the right hand* |
| **Dan** | *Judge* |
| **Naphtali** | *Firmness; strength* |
| **Gad** | *Good fortune* |
| **Asher** | *Happiness and blessing* |

These names deliver a very compelling message about a Son we will see, whom we should hear, be attached to, and celebrate, who will bring a reward and inhabit His people, be a tender branch, Son of the right hand, a Judge with strength, and who will bring goodness, happiness, and blessing.

### Remind you of anyone?

The Son, of course, is the glorious Messiah Yahshua (Jesus)! When I first saw the definitions of these names, you could have knocked me over with a feather. The Messiah was foretold even in the very names God gave to Israel's twelve tribes!

What a stunning revelation!

## WHO IS THE LORD?

As believers in the LORD, we must absolutely know who this God is that we worship and serve. Today's worldwide culture worships countless gods, lords, and idols. A few years ago, I was watching a movie, and there was a group of people worshiping their lord, singing praises to him, and fervently expressing how much they adored the lord.

When they finally spoke the name of their "lord," I was astonished that it was not the name of the God I serve within the Judeo-Christian faith; it was the name of a widely worshiped deity in one of the world's other major religions. I mistakenly thought they were worshiping the God of Abraham, Isaac, and Jacob, but I was terribly wrong.

After seeing this movie, a fire ignited within me, and I began to passionately pursue and inquire of God regarding His name. I was convicted and convinced that I had to know the specific, unique, personal name of the one true and living God recorded in the Old Testament as "the LORD."

## THE NAME OF THE LORD REVEALED

The first time the name of the LORD, Yahweh, is revealed in Scripture is in the second chapter of Genesis.

*This is the account of heaven and earth when they were created, at the time when* **Yahweh Elohim** *made earth and heaven. (Genesis 2:4 NOG)*

The word "elohim" is the plural form of "el," which is the Hebrew word for "mighty one," or "god." In ancient times, the terms el and elohim were not only used to describe the one true living God, Yahweh. El and elohim were also used by many nations to describe their pagan gods. The Egyptians, for example, worshiped ten false gods.

Since the titles of el and elohim could refer to countless gods among the pagans, God instructed His servant Moses, in Exodus 3:15, to use the specific name of Yahweh when speaking about Him to others. In this way, the LORD ensured that there would be no confusion about who sent Moses to speak to Pharaoh and which God would be rescuing Israel and delivering them <u>out</u> of bondage and <u>into</u> freedom!

> *Again **Elohim** said to Moses, "This is what you must say to the people of Israel: **Yahweh Elohim** of your ancestors, the **Elohim** of Abraham, Isaac, and Jacob, has sent me to you. This is my name forever. This is my title throughout every generation." (NOG)*

In the book of Isaiah, Yahweh again makes very clear His distinct personal name that is His and His alone.

> *I am **Yahweh**; that is my name. I will not give my glory to anyone else or the praise I deserve to idols. (Isaiah 42:8 NOG)*

Here we see that Yahweh is ensuring that His glory will not be attributed to false gods or idols. This is one reason why His specific personal name is recorded thousands of times in Scripture; yet, in most English translations of the Bible, wherever the name Yahweh should appear, it has been replaced with the word LORD. The original

**The name Yahweh is recorded thousands of times in Scripture.**

Hebrew text, on the other hand, records the name Yahweh as the Tetragrammaton יהוה. (The term "Tetragrammaton" is the Greek word for the four Hebrew letters Yod-Hey-Waw-Hey, YHWH, or Yahweh. Please note that Hebrew is read right to left rather than left to right, as English is read.)

The Hebrew language is a very rich and fascinating language. In ancient times, the Hebrew alphabet was illustrated in pictures or pictographs; therefore, each Hebrew letter actually represented a word or words.

To give you an example of one of the differences between English and Hebrew, our English alphabet (A, B, C, D, etc.) contains 26 letters that in and of themselves mean nothing; however, the Hebrew alphabet (alef, beit, gimmel, dalet, etc.) contains 22 letters which are pictographs that represent words. For instance, the Hebrew letter alef is illustrated by the pictograph of an ox and signifies strength. The Hebrew letter beit (pronounced bait) is represented by the pictograph of a house or dwelling. Each letter of the Hebrew alphabet has a distinct meaning.

Now, knowing that Hebrew letters actually tell a story, let's look very closely at each of the letters that form Yahweh's name, Yod-Hey-Waw-Hey (YHWH).

The pictograph for Yod looks like an arm or **hand** that is suspended in mid-air. י

The pictograph for Hey resembles a window, and means look, see, or **behold**. ה

The pictograph for Waw resembles a tent peg, and means hook or **nail**. ו

When we put the meaning of the letters that form Yahweh's name in a sentence, His name declares, "Behold the hand, behold the nail!" יהוה

**Yahshua (Jesus) is revealed in the very name of YHWH!** When Yahweh revealed His name to Moses as Israel's Redeemer from the physical bondage of slavery, embedded within His name was the revelation of Messiah Yahshua as the Redeemer of those enslaved to the spiritual bondage of sin.

Because there is such a deep, powerful meaning in the name of Yahweh, it's obvious that He never intended it to be hidden. Let's look at His powerful name when coupled with some of His characteristics and titles of position. The following list contains just a few of Yahweh's attributes and titles, with His name listed first, followed by a Hebrew word describing a characteristic or title, and then the English translation of that attribute in parentheses.

Yahweh Adonai (Lord)
Yahweh Elohim (God)
Yahweh Goel (Redeemer)
Yahweh Yireh (Provider)
Yahweh Rapha (Healer)
Yahweh Nissi (Banner)
Yahweh Shalom (Peace)
Yahweh Rohe (Shepherd)
Yahweh Tsidkenu (Righteousness)
Yahweh Shammah (Present)
Yahweh Elyon (Most High)
Yahweh M'Kaddesh (Sanctifier)
Yahweh Yahshua (Salvation)

When Moses asked God His name, He replied, "EHYEH ASHER EHYEH," which means, "I am and will be who I am and will be." God was assuring Moses that He would be everything he needed in that present moment and in his future. However, when speaking His name to others, Moses could not say EHYEH, because God is the only one who can say "I am and will be" of Himself. What He told Moses to say was, "He is now and forever will be who He is and will be," which is the name we call Him, Yahweh.

Every time we proclaim His name, we are declaring, in faith, "He is now and forever will be." Now just think of the power produced when we couple His name with His many attributes. We get a triumphant declaration of not only who He is, but a proclamation of in whom we have total confidence, trust, assurance, and faith, and to whom we pledge our allegiance.

> **He is now and forever will be...**

For instance, when we say Yahweh Goel, we are proclaiming, "He is now and forever will be Redeemer!" Declare Yahweh Yireh, and we're crying out, "He is now and forever will be Provider!" If you desire peace, proclaim, Yahweh Shalom, "He is now and forever will be Peace!"

Yahweh's name not only testifies of His might and power; it also testifies of His faithfulness. He does not change. He is the same yesterday, today, and forever. That means He is faithful today, tomorrow, and forever. He is peace today, tomorrow, and forever. He is present today, tomorrow, and forever. His name solidifies that

He will not change, and we can absolutely trust Him today, tomorrow, and forever!

*Yahshua Messiah (Yahweh with us) the same yesterday, and to day, and for ever. (Hebrews 13:8 RSB)*

The Word of God encourages us to exalt, magnify, and praise the name of Yahweh. On the other hand, the enemy of our souls is trying very hard to keep His name the world's best kept secret. We are warned by God not to use His name vainly, idly, carelessly, nor profanely, but Yahweh never instructed us to hide His name.

## TITLE VERSUS NAME

The term "lord" is a generic title and is used to describe a position of authority. A lord is defined as a master or ruler; someone or something having power, control, authority, or influence. Interestingly, the title "lord" is still used today to describe members of the peerage in the United Kingdom. (The peerage is a legal system of largely hereditary titles of British nobility in the United Kingdom.)

Because Yahweh is our Master, the title LORD is appropriate, but that is not His name. Remember, the very name of Yahweh declares, "He is now and forever will be who He is and will be."

Although the title LORD makes a powerful statement about His position, it does not fully describe and acknowledge Him as the one and only faithful, eternal, boundless, limitless, inexhaustible, infinite God, nor does the title LORD distinguish Him from the countless lords, gods, and idols that are worshiped around the world today.

The term "god" is also a generic term that means "mighty one." People in ancient times assigned the terms "lord" and "god" to false gods, such as Baal, Asherah, Dagon, Molech, Tammuz, etc. These entities were assigned power through the minds of people, who then gave them physical features in the form of statues; nonetheless, these "gods" had no real power.

*Their idols are made of silver and gold. They were made by human hands. They have mouths, but they cannot speak. They have eyes, but they cannot see. They have ears, but they cannot hear. They have noses, but they cannot smell. They have hands, but they cannot feel. They have feet, but they cannot walk. They cannot even make a sound with their throats. Those who make idols end up like them. So does everyone who trusts them. (Psalm 115:4-8 NOG)*

In ancient Greece, Yahweh was lumped together and accepted alongside Apollo, Poseidon, Zeus, and a myriad of other gods. There was even a Greek god named Chaos. Of course, absolute chaos is what you get when you lump and mix Yahweh with gods of luck, magic, mythology, nature worship, etc.

Satan wants the world to be chaotic, disordered, confusing, and dark. He doesn't want people to know the difference between darkness and light or the difference between Yahweh and the multitude of other gods and idols that people worship.

Some within our modern culture worship idols that have an abundance of influence, but no genuine divine power. Today's idols include movie stars, music celebrities, money, material possessions, and even false gods associated with weather, animals, and nature.

It's important to note that there is a dangerous trend taking place among Christians, today. Since Yahweh's name is largely unknown by most people, there are some Christians who mistakenly believe that Christians and Muslims worship the same God; however, nothing could be further from the truth. When we read the Word of God with the divine name Yahweh restored to its original place in the Scriptures, we begin to see a depiction of Yahweh and Yahshua that do not resemble Allah at all. Furthermore, in the nearly 7,000 times that Yahweh's name is revealed in His sacred Word, not one time does He ever refer to Himself as Allah.

Yahweh is distinctive, and no other god or idol can make the claim that they are the Creator of all things, that they are eternal, or that they are life, light, and love. Yahweh alone is the Savior and Redeemer of those who <u>believe in His name</u>. The one true living God is Yahweh, and we must exalt, glorify, magnify, and praise **His** holy name!

## DO NOT TAKE YAHWEH'S NAME IN VAIN

Astonishingly, the name of Yahweh has been blotted out and replaced by the title LORD over 6,800 times in the Tanakh, which is commonly referred to as the Old Testament. By replacing Yahweh with LORD, translators have blatantly violated Yahweh's command given in Exodus 20:7.

Let's review Exodus 20:7 in the *King James (KJV), The Scriptures (ISR), The Names of God (NOG),* and the *Restoration Study Bible (RSB)* translations:

18

*Thou shalt not take the name of the LORD thy God in vain; for the LORD will not hold him guiltless that taketh his name in vain. (KJV)*

*You do not bring the Name of יהוה (Yahweh) your Elohim to naught, for יהוה does not leave the one unpunished who brings His Name to naught. (ISR)*

*Never use the name of **Yahweh** your **Elohim** carelessly. **Yahweh** will make sure that anyone who carelessly uses his name will be punished. (NOG)*

*Thou shalt not take the name of Yahweh thy Elohim in vain; for Yahweh will not hold him guiltless that taketh his name in vain. (RSB)*

As you can see, the *King James* translation deletes Yahweh's name from the biblical text; however, *The Scriptures, The Names of God,* and the *Restoration Study Bible* translations restore the name Yahweh, in keeping with the original Hebrew text.

The word *vain* is defined as producing no result, being fruitless, useless, pointless, hopeless, and worthless. By this definition, I believe Yahweh is instructing us to use His name appropriately; therefore, we are never to use His name in an evil and destructive way nor in a useless and pointless way.

By issuing the decree, *"Thou shalt not take the name of Yahweh thy Elohim in vain,"* Yahweh is <u>not</u> commanding us to blot out His name from Scripture nor from our vocabulary; instead, He is instructing us to speak His name with the utmost reverence and respect.

Yahweh's name should never be flippantly blurted out nor thoughtlessly uttered. His name should not be spoken out as some magic word that fixes everything. Speaking His name is a very serious matter and when spoken appropriately, the very mention of His name bears fruit and is effective and powerful!

*The Scriptures* translation of Exodus 20:7 declares we should never bring Yahweh's name to naught, to nothing, having no purpose and no effect.

*You do not bring the Name of יהוה your Elohim to naught, for יהוה does not leave the one unpunished who brings His Name to naught. (ISR)*

In the *King James* translation, this verse refers to the "name of the LORD," but then conceals and blots out the original Hebrew text, which records the LORD's name, Yahweh. Changing the Scripture verse from Yahweh to LORD denies the power of God's name and brings it to naught, to nothing, because it has been eradicated. We are

**Do not add to nor take away from the Word of God.**

cautioned in both Old and New Testaments to never add to nor take away from the divinely-inspired Word of God.

*Do not add to the Word which I command you, and do not take away from it, so as to guard the commands of יהוה (Yahweh) your Elohim which I am commanding you. (Deuteronomy 4:2 ISR)*

*All the words I am commanding you, guard to do it – and do not add to it nor take away from it. (Deuteronomy 12:32 ISR)*

*What is His Name, and what is His Son's Name, if you know it? Every Word of Eloah is tried; He is a shield to those taking refuge in Him. Do not add to His Words, lest He reprove you, and you be found a liar. (Proverbs 30:4b-6 ISR)*

*For I witness to everyone hearing the words of the prophecy of this book: If anyone adds to them, Elohim shall add to him the plagues that are written in this book, and if anyone takes away from the words of the book of this prophecy, Elohim shall take away his part from the Book of Life, and out of the set-apart city, which are written in this Book. (Revelation 22:18-19 ISR)*

Yahweh's name <u>must not</u> be removed from His Word nor from our lips; and although the passage in Revelation 22:18-19 speaks specifically about the book of Revelation, I believe it would do us well to apply this resounding admonition to <u>all</u> Scripture.

By erasing, blotting out, and obliterating Yahweh's name from Scripture and from our vocabulary, the adversary (Satan) succeeds in making us weak and impotent.

*Having a form of holiness, but denying the power thereof... (2 Timothy 3:5a RSB)*

We must not allow Satan to eradicate Yahweh's name from the very Scriptures He so lovingly authored. The Creator of the universe desires for us to know Him in a personal and intimate way, so we must speak His name and not just His titles. Anyone can say, "Lord, Lord," as Yahshua warned us; but it doesn't mean they are calling on the one true God, Yahweh.

> *Not every one that saith unto me, Lord, Lord, shall enter into the kingdom of heaven; but he that doeth the will of my Father which is in heaven. Many will say to me in that day, Lord, Lord, have we not prophesied in thy name? and in thy name have cast out devils? and in thy name done many wonderful works? And then will I profess unto them, I never knew you: depart from me, ye that work iniquity. (Matthew 7:21-23 KJV)*

Let's be specific about whom we worship. Many are calling out, "Lord, Lord." Believers must ensure that all of heaven and earth know whom we are calling upon: the one and only true and living God, Yahweh.

Using Yahweh's name appropriately, as He has instructed us, gives Him the glory, honor, and respect He deserves and sets Him apart from the countless false gods, lords, and idols worshiped – past, present, and future.

> *Not unto us, O Yahweh, not unto us, but unto thy name give glory, for thy mercy, and for thy truth's sake. (Psalm 115:1 RSB)*

## THE LORD OUR GOD, YAHWEH, IS ONE!

The name of the LORD is also recorded in Scripture as Yah, the short form of Yahweh. When I speak or read the name of Yah, I think of Yahweh, Yahshua (Jesus), and the Ruach HaKodesh (Holy Spirit) as one, or the

Hebrew word *echad*, which means one, united, altogether, or alike.

> *Hear, O Israel: Yahweh our Elohim is one Yahweh: And thou shalt love Yahweh thy Elohim with all thine heart, and with all thy soul, and with all thy might. (Deuteronomy 6:4-5 RSB)*

> *Hear, O Israel: the **LORD our God is one LORD**: (emphasis added) And thou shalt love the LORD thy God with all thine heart, and with all thy soul, and with all thy might. (Deuteronomy 6:4-5 KJV)*

> *People may say that there are gods in heaven and on earth—many gods and many lords, as they would call them. But for us, "There is only **one God** (emphasis added), the Father. Everything came from him, and we live for him. There is only **one Lord** (emphasis added), **Yeshua** Christ. Everything came into being through him, and we live because of him." (1 Corinthians 8:5-6 NOG)*

Even though the *King James* version of Deuteronomy 6:4-5 omits the name Yahweh, I've included this version to make a point. We know that everywhere the Old Testament records LORD in the *King James*, it should actually say Yahweh. When the Old Testament was translated from Hebrew to Greek (The Septuagint), the word *Kurios* was substituted to represent Yahweh's name. Now, understanding that Kurios is the Greek word used for Yahweh, we can read the passage in 1 Corinthians 8:6, "But for us, there is only one God, the Father. Everything came from Him, and we live for Him. There is only one Yahweh, Jesus

Christ (Yahshua the Messiah). Everything came into being through him, and we live because of Him."

Wow! What an astounding statement! Yahweh is Yahshua! Now, since we know that Yahweh and Yahshua are one, we can be assured that calling on the name Yahweh is the same as calling on the name Yahshua. There is neither discord, dispute, nor conflict between Yahweh, Yahshua, and the Holy Spirit; and there is no division of Elohim's will, purpose, authority, and power within God.

**Yahweh and Yahshua are One!**

In Psalm 68:4 (NOG), the name Yah is referred to as Elohim, the plural form of El (God). This, for me, is another confirmation that Yahweh, Yahshua, and the Holy Spirit are one.

*Sing to Elohim; make music to praise his name. Make a highway for him to ride through the deserts. Yah is his name. Celebrate in his presence.*

Yahweh, Yahshua, and the Holy Spirit are three manifestations or expressions of one all-knowing, all-powerful, forgiving, merciful, just, loving, and righteous God. There are not three Gods; there is only one God.

Yahshua the Messiah is not a separate person from Yahweh. He is God in the flesh, who came to redeem mankind by becoming our Passover Lamb. Yahshua is the physical expression of Yahweh that could be seen and beheld as His ultimate expression of love.

In our current sinful human condition, we cannot look upon the complete radiance and full presence of

Yahweh, or we would die. The purity and holiness of God would consume us. In our current earthbound state, we can only see the Messiah manifestation of Yahweh, His right hand, so to speak, sent to save and rescue us from sin. Understand, though, that Yahshua is not merely Yahweh's right hand or just an agent of Yahweh. Yahshua is Yahweh revealed to us.

*Your right hand, O יהוה, has become great in power. Your right hand, O יהוה, has crushed the enemy. (Exodus 15:6 ISR)*

*But you can't see my face, because no one may see me and live. (Exodus 33:20 NOG)*

*For now we see in a mirror, dimly, but then face to face. Now I know in part, but then I shall know, as I also have been known. (1 Corinthians 13:12 ISR)*

## GOD WITH US

Yahweh entered this sin-infected earth realm wrapped in flesh and blood as Yahshua, to then live under the very laws, ordinances, and instructions that He Himself had issued to mankind. In Yahshua, He came to not only demonstrate, up close and personal, how to live a victorious life here on earth; He came to reclaim the keys of death and hell that Adam relinquished to the enemy long ago in the Garden of Eden. After paying the sacrificial price for mankind with His shed blood, Yahshua boldly proclaimed:

*I am the first and the last, the living one. I was dead, but now I am alive forever. I have the keys of death and hell. (Revelation 1:17b-18 NOG)*

Yahweh in the flesh, Yahshua, became the sacrificial Lamb of God, slain for the sin of the world, and the Redeemer who would regain His treasured possession, His people, for His very own, if only they would believe.

*For Elohim so loved the world that He gave His only brought-forth Son, so that everyone who believes in Him should not perish but possess everlasting life. (John 3:16 ISR)*

We can only come to Yahweh through Yahshua; and when we behold Yahshua, we behold Yahweh, for they are one. Yahshua explains it beautifully in the book of John.

*__Yeshua__[1] answered him, "I am the way, the truth, and the life. No one goes to the Father except through me. If you have known me, you will also know my Father. From now on you know him through me and have seen him in me." Philip said to __Yeshua__, "Lord, show us the Father, and that will satisfy us." __Yeshua__ replied, "I have been with all of you for a long time. Don't you know me yet, Philip? The person who has seen me has seen the Father. So how can you say, 'Show us the Father'? Don't you believe that I am in the Father and the Father is in me? What I'm telling you doesn't come from me. The Father, who lives in me, does what he wants. Believe me when I say that I am in the Father and that the Father is in me. Otherwise,*

---

[1] *The Names of God Bible* editors prefer to spell the Messiah's name as Yeshua rather than Yahshua. See the section titled, "At the Name of Jesus..." on page 32 for more information on the spelling of the Messiah's name.

*believe me because of the things I do." (John 14:6-11 NOG)*

God the Father, Yahweh, has brought about salvation for mankind through faith in God the Son, Yahshua, so that we can live in paradise, the renewed Jerusalem, the restored Garden of Eden, forever and ever!

## IT'S ALL ABOUT RELATIONSHIP

The relationship of Yahweh, Yahshua, and the Holy Spirit is a beautiful picture of the relationship Elohim desires to have with His people. We are to be one, as He is one. Yahshua's prayer to Abba (Father) Yahweh, on behalf of believers, is a very powerful depiction of all relationships.

*"And I do not pray for these alone, but also for those believing in Me through their word, so that they all might be one, as You, Father, are in Me, and I in You, so that they too might be one in Us, so that the world might believe that You have sent Me. And the esteem which You gave Me I have given them, so that they might be one as We are one, I in them, and You in Me, so that they might be perfected into one, so that the world knows that You have sent Me, and have loved them as You have loved Me. Father, I desire that those whom You have given Me, might be with Me where I am, so that they see My esteem which You have given Me, because You loved Me before the foundation of the world. O righteous Father, indeed the world did not know You, but I knew You, and these knew that You sent Me. **And I have made Your Name**</*

*known to them, and shall make it known*
*(emphasis added), so that the love with which You*
*loved Me might be in them, and I in them." (John*
*17:20-26 ISR)*

This passage of Scripture may be confusing, if read only in a literal sense and relying on our own understanding; but if read with an understanding given by the Holy Spirit about the symbolism contained in this divine mystery, the meaning becomes clear. Yahshua is describing His relationship with Yahweh as a relationship of One: Yahshua living in Yahweh and Yahweh living in Yahshua. He then goes on to express His desire that His body of believers will also walk in that same oneness figuratively as Yahweh and Yahshua are One literally.

Besides demonstrating relationship, this passage of Scripture speaks about the name of God. The last thing Yahshua communicates in this compelling prayer about relationship is that He has revealed the name of His Father, Yahweh, to those He is leaving behind, so that the love of the Father will be in them, and Yahshua will remain in them.

In another passage of Scripture, the writer of Hebrews acknowledges that Yahweh and Yahshua are One and that Yahshua made Yahweh's name known to His brothers.

*For both He who sets apart and those who are*
*being set apart are all of One, for which reason He*
*is not ashamed to call them brothers, saying, "I*
*shall announce Your Name to My brothers,*
*(emphasis added) in the midst of the congregation*
*I shall sing praise to You." (Hebrews 2:11-12 ISR)*

Hebrews 2:12 is clearly referring to a passage in the Psalms written by David when he was under attack from his enemies.

*I make known Your Name to My brothers; In the midst of the assembly I praise You. (Psalm 22:22 ISR)*

During Yahshua's ministry, the ban against speaking Yahweh's name was already in effect, instituted by the religious leaders, and it was considered blasphemy to utter the name of the Almighty. Yahshua, however, came to restore all things, including the name of His Father; therefore, Yahshua made His Father's name known. Because of the ban on speaking the Name, the English translation of the New Testament does not record Yahweh's name; nevertheless, it is evident that Yahshua spoke His Father's name and did not suppress it.

## ESTABLISHING A CONNECTION

Up to this point, I hope I have made it clear that names are very important. Knowing a person's name is especially important when trying to connect with them. It's very difficult to establish a personal relationship or make a connection with someone if you don't know their name. One of the first things we do when meeting a new person is to introduce ourselves by name and then ask the person we're meeting for their name.

Even when we are introduced to someone by a third party, we are, of course, introduced by name. Once introduced, if we forget the name of someone we might be interested in knowing better and with whom we'd like to establish a friendship or relationship, we make sure that we ask for their name again. It is nearly impossible to have a close relationship with someone if we don't know their name.

Suppressing the name of Yahweh is similar to a wife refusing to call her husband by his specific name and only addressing him by the generic term "husband." Imagine how hurt you would be if your spouse or even your best friend refused to address you by your specific personal name and insisted on calling you by the vague generic term "human" when speaking to you or about you.

Relationships cannot be established and maintained if we cannot show respect by speaking distinct personal names when addressing our friends, family, neighbors, coworkers, etc. Likewise, we fail to honor God when we refuse to call Him by His unique personal name, the name He lovingly unveiled almost 7,000 times in His Word.

When we call on the name Yahweh, we offer korban (the Hebrew word for a sacrificial gift brought near the altar). The word korban literally means to draw near to God. Yahweh's revelation of His name to us in Scripture is a gift, and to call on His name is to show appreciation for His gift, as we approach Him with the sacrifice of praise.

> *By him therefore let us offer the sacrifice of praise to Elohim continually, that is the fruit of our lips* ***giving thanks to his name***. *(emphasis added) (Hebrews 13:15 RSB)*

Yahweh, our highest authority, the Most High God, desires a personal relationship with His people, and so He has revealed His name thousands of times throughout Scripture. There is nothing wrong with acknowledging His authority, title, and position by calling Him God or LORD, but we must not abandon His holy name (Yahweh) or the name of His only begotten Son (Yahshua).

## FRIEND OR ACQUAINTANCE?

Once we establish a relationship with someone, there is a big difference between a friend and an acquaintance. While an acquaintance is someone we know casually, a friend is someone to whom we are attached, devoted, and committed. It's my desire to know Yahweh as Abraham knew Him, as a friend.

*And the scripture was fulfilled which saith, ABRAHAM BELIEVED YAHWEH, AND IT WAS IMPUTED UNTO HIM FOR RIGHTEOUSNESS: and he was called the Friend of Yahweh. (James 2:23 RSB)*

When we have a close relationship with someone, we call them by their name, and they call us by our name. There is no distance, separation, or barrier built between friends by refusing to call one another personally by name.

I know of a man and woman who were going through a very rough time in their marriage, and divorce was imminent. They barely spoke to one another; and when the husband spoke to his wife, he was cold and withdrawn, and would not speak her name under any circumstance.

He was in an adulterous relationship with another woman; and, apparently, he was proving some sort of ridiculous point to himself and the other woman that his marriage was emotionally over by refusing to speak his wife's name. Of course, the adultery and lack of communication brought the marriage to its ultimate demise, and their marital bond was severed once and for all.

Don't throw up a wall in your relationship with Yahweh by refusing to speak His name.

## AT THE NAME OF JESUS...

So far, I've emphasized the importance of Yahweh's name and touched lightly on the name of Yahshua the Messiah. Now let's discuss the name of Jesus. Where does His name fit into this dynamic? Well, through the years, the Messiah's name has been transliterated into many languages, such as Greek (Ieosus, pronounced ee-ay-sooce), Latin (Iesus), and modern-day English (Jesus). However, if we look at the original Hebrew language, we find that the Savior's name is Yahshua.

Jesus is a transliteration of Yahshua, not a translation. A translation takes a word or group of words from one language and converts those words to another language. A transliteration takes a letter and converts it to a similar letter in a different language. So, if the Hebrew name Yahshua were translated into English it would be Salvation; but since Jesus is a transliteration, each letter of Yahshua is converted to similar letters within the English language, forming the name Jesus.

Spoiler Alert: Contrary to what many may believe, the first appearance of the name of Jesus (Yahshua) is not in Matthew. The first occurrence of the word *salvation* (yshuwah), and therefore the first mention of Yahshua is in the book of Genesis.

*I have waited for thy salvation (Yahshua), O Yahweh. (Genesis 49:18 RSB)*

It's so incredible that the Hebrew name for Jesus (Yahshua) actually contains within it the Hebrew word for salvation. *Strong's Concordance* records the word for salvation as yshuwah (pronounced yesh-oo-aw), #H3444.

I believe that when Yahweh revealed the name of His Son to Joseph and Mary, He pronounced it in Hebrew, since that was the language Joseph and Mary, as Hebrews, would have spoken.

*Joseph had this in mind when an angel of the Lord appeared to him in a dream. The angel said to him, "Joseph, descendant of David, don't be afraid to take Mary as your wife. She is pregnant by the Holy Spirit. She will give birth to a son, and you will name him **Yeshua** [He Saves], because he will save his people from their sins." (Matthew 1:20-21 NOG)*

In documents printed in the English language, you will see the Messiah's Hebrew name spelled as Yeshua or Yahshua. I prefer Yahshua, because to me it specifies from whom salvation has come, Yahweh. Yahshua literally means Yah is Salvation. Even though there may be varying opinions on the spelling of Yahshua, I don't think that the

> **Yah Is Salvation**

spelling of our Savior's name should be a point of contention or a cause for discord in the body of Christ. I think that we should be gracious enough toward one another that our opinions, based on faithful study, do not cause dissension in the body.

If we pronounce and spell our Savior's name as Yeshua, it is fine, because Strong's H3444 is yshuwah, meaning salvation, deliverance, healing, help, security, victory, aid, well-being, and prosperity. If we pronounce and spell the Messiah's name as Yahshua, it's fine, also, because Yah stands for "He is now and forever will be who He is and will be," and shua means "freedom and wealth." So either way, the Savior and Messiah's name is a declaration of total victory!

Please note that the wealth in shua refers to the spiritual <u>and</u> physical abundant life Yahshua promised.

*I am the door: by me if any man enter in, he shall be saved, and shall go in and out, and find pasture. The thief cometh not, but for to steal, and to kill, and to destroy: I am come that they might have life, and that they might have it more abundantly. (John 10:9-10 RSB)*

*I am the gate. Those who enter the sheep pen through me will be saved. They will go in and out of the sheep pen and find food. A thief comes to steal, kill, and destroy. But I came so that my sheep will have life and so that they will have everything they need. (John 10:9-10 NOG)*

As I mentioned earlier, the Hebrew language is a very rich language, and each letter symbolically represents a word, words, or a concept. I bring this up here, again, because the preceding verse points out that Yahshua is the door or the gate to enter into life.

Yahshua is the Good Shepherd of His sheep, Israel, and also the Shepherd of those who have been grafted into Israel, those who follow Christ. So Israel and those grafted into Israel, by the blood of Yahshua, and belief in His sacrificial atonement, and who accept Yahshua as Savior and Lord are part of Israel and can enter into life through Him.

The interesting thing is that the Good Shepherd Yahshua is from the tribe of Judah and is also called the Lion of the Tribe of Judah, or Yehudah in Hebrew. Yehudah is spelled Yod-Hey-Waw-Dalet-Hey in the Hebrew alphabet. You can see that the name of Yahweh, Yod-Hey-Waw-Hey, is contained within the name of His people. That alone is enough to make you jump up and shout! But there's more.

One letter is added into Yahweh's name to form the name of His people, the dalet, which is a pictograph of a door. Yod-Hey-Waw-Hey has made a way for His people to enter through the Door, Yahshua. So, the Door, Yahshua, is in His name, Yahweh, so that His people can enter into eternal life. The Hebrew letter dalet, the door, is within the name of His people, Yehudah, Yod-Hey-Waw-Dalet-Hey, ה ד ו ה י. Embedded within the name of Yahweh's people, Yehudah, Yahweh is crying out, "Yehudah, behold the hand, behold the nail, behold the Door!"

Let's be very clear. Yahweh chose Israel as His people, but that alone does not save them, for we have all sinned and fallen short of the glory of Yah. Salvation isn't through genealogy; salvation is obtained by going through the Door, through belief in Yahshua.

I would encourage everyone to begin to study Hebrew and the rich, fertile soil and roots that we, as followers of Yahshua, have in the Hebrew faith. I have learned so much through searching for my spiritual roots. The Holy Spirit is opening up an understanding of the character and nature of Yahweh that I never dreamed was possible, and this book is only scratching the surface of what He has in store for us when we actually dwell and abide in His name. As Proverbs 18:10 declares, Yahweh's name is a strong tower that the righteous run into and are safe. Well, we don't have to run in and out of safety; we can dwell in His name. His name is not just a word that I speak; His name is the place where I dwell.

> **Yahweh's name is not just a word that I speak; His name is the place where I dwell.**

*He that dwelleth in the secret place of the most High shall abide under the shadow of the Almighty. I will say of Yahweh, He is my refuge and my fortress: my Elohim; in him will I trust. (Psalm 91:1-2 RSB)*

In my opinion, the secret place of the Most High God where we can abide in safety is in His name!

Let's go back to John 10:9-10 for a moment. Another valuable lesson we get from this passage is that Yahshua points out we will have abundant life and everything we need through Him. Yahshua means Yah's freedom and wealth. Yah represents Yahweh, of course, and shua represents freedom and wealth. The wealth in the definition of shua, however, is not defined as the greed that pervades our society, where people cannot get enough money, no matter how much they accumulate and amass. That is the very definition of "the love of money, which is the root of all evil," which Scripture warns against.

*For the love of money is a root of all kinds of evil, for which some, by longing for it, have strayed from the belief, and pierced themselves through with many pains. (1 Timothy 6:10 ISR)*

Love is defined as an intense feeling of deep affection. In the extreme, love of something can be defined as "a deep yearning, wherein you are unable to get enough." So, as referenced in the above Scripture, I believe love of money is defined as not being able to get enough money. No matter how much you have, it is not enough. You desire more and more. You can't be content with what you have, and you are greedy and want to amass more and more money and material things. What Yahweh blesses you with cannot satisfy, and you continually covet, yearn, and long for more.

We are to love Yahweh, yearn and long for Him to the point that we feel we can't get enough of Him. We are not to yearn for and covet money and things. Of course, if we long for Yahweh, we are also longing for Yahshua, the Messiah manifestation of Yahweh, who died for our sin, who is our freedom and liberty.

Let's take a look at *Strong's Concordance* numbers H7768, H7769, and H7771 to gain an understanding of the shua portion of Yahshua's name. Note that there is not one *Strong's* number that defines shua. We must look at three references to get the full meaning.

When we look at these three references, we find that shua is defined in *Strong's* H7768/7769 as, "cry aloud for help and freedom," and *Strong's* H7771 is defined as wealth and liberality. We know that the Yah in Yahshua stands for, "He is," which is the first three letters of Yahweh. So, when we call on Yahshua, we are crying out and saying, "He is help, He is freedom, and He is liberal and generous."

Again, I cannot stress enough that Yah is contained in the names of Yahweh and Yahshua. Yahshua's name is written in Hebrew as יהושע Yod-Hey-Waw-Shin-Ayin. You can see that the first three letters of Yahshua are the same as the first three letters of Yahweh יהוה, Yod-Hey-Waw, pronounced Yah. (Remember, Hebrew is read right to left.)

It is so very crucial to comprehend this fact, because it will fortify your spirit and bolster your confidence in the reality that Yahshua came in His Father's name and authority and that He is the Door to freedom! Yahshua is not a separate person from Yahweh. He is Yahweh, who came in the flesh to rescue and redeem us. We can't be like the religious leaders of Yahshua's day, who denied His identity, authority, and power.

*I am come in my Father's name, and ye receive me not: if another shall come in his own name, him ye will receive. (John 5:43 RSB)*

*יהושע (Yahshua) answered them, "I have told you, and you do not believe. The works that I do in My Father's Name, they bear witness concerning Me." (John 10:25 ISR)*

We must know beyond any shadow of doubt that Yahshua came in His Father's name and authority, and we must resolve deep within our hearts to submit to Yahshua the Son as to Yahweh the Father. Just as Yahshua came in His Father's name and authority, the believer today must be confident in knowing that when we come in the name of Yah, we come in the authority of Yah!

*Who has gone up to the heavens and come down? Who has gathered the wind in His fists? Who has bound the waters in a garment? Who established all the ends of the earth? What is His Name, and what is His Son's Name, if you know it? (Proverbs 30:4 ISR)*

*"See, I am sending a Messenger before you to guard you in the way and to bring you into the place which I have prepared. Be on guard before Him and obey His voice. Do not rebel against Him, for He is not going to pardon your transgression, for My Name is in Him." (Exodus 23:20-21 ISR)*

Let me put it in modern terms. Just as the son of a man named John Smith would more than likely have Smith as part of his name, I believe Yahweh's name is contained within the name of His Son, Yahshua. Perhaps that's one of the reasons Yahweh revealed His unique relationship with Yahshua within the distinct bond of Father and Son.

Yahshua is a reflection of Yahweh. When we call on the name of Yahshua, we call on the name of Yahweh. We're crying out, "Yah, save and deliver!" What a marvelous revelation of the power of Yah's name!

The prophet Joel proclaimed:

*Then whoever calls on the name of **Yahweh** will be saved. Those who escape will be on Mount Zion and in Jerusalem. Among the survivors will be those whom **Yahweh** calls, as **Yahweh** has promised. (Joel 2:32 NOG)*

In Acts, the Apostle Peter declares:

*And it shall be that everyone who calls on the Name of* יהוה *shall be saved. (Acts 2:21 ISR)*

You may be wondering, "Why all the emphasis on the names of Yahweh and Yahshua and stressing that they are one?" Because within the name of Yah is a simple, yet very potent reality: Yahweh's miraculous power and presence can be revealed in any way He desires, and He has chosen to release His power at the mention of His name, because that releases His sovereign authority and power. Again, to come in the name of Yah means we come in the authority of Yah!

Yahshua is the bridge between time and eternity. At the mention of Yahweh Yahshua, He shatters the boundaries of time and space. No matter what circumstance dominates your life, right now, He wants you to know that He is ever present and more than able to bring you victory.

Remember, within His compound names, He is not only Yahweh Yireh (Provider); He is Yahweh Yahshua (Salvation). He's not only Yahweh Rapha (Healer); He is Yahweh Tsidkenu (Righteousness). If you need peace, He is Yahweh Shalom. If you need direction, He is Yahweh Rohe, the Good Shepherd who is leading you through the dark night. He is Yahweh Goel, our mighty Redeemer!

Yahweh came in the flesh in the person of Yahshua to redeem us and rescue us from sin and give us eternal life. To paraphrase a dear friend of mine, "The Creator came to rescue His creation."

## OPPOSITES DO NOT ATTRACT

Now that we've explored the definition of *name*, let's touch briefly on its antonym. An antonym is a word opposite in meaning to another. For example, the antonym for hot is cold; the antonym for good is bad.

Antonyms for *name* include nouns such as anonymous, nameless, nobody, nonentity, and verbs such as reject, denounce, conceal, and suppress. Get the picture? Satan is diabolically trying to overcome the power of the believer by hiding Yahweh's name. Even the adversary knows there is salvation, deliverance, freedom, and power in the mighty name of Yah!

The aforementioned antonyms clearly describe the enemy's plan to eradicate the name of Yahweh and wipe it from memory; consequently, we, as believers, must not suppress Yahweh's name, abandon it, nor make it indistinct and trivial. How abhorrent it is to make Yahweh's name meaningless and devoid of power, the very name He revealed to us thousands of times in Scripture, so that we could identify personally with Him, the one true and living God!

Yahweh loves you so much, that He gave His life to give you eternal life with Him. He longs to have a loving, intimate relationship with you, and He longs to hear you call His name.

יהוה

# Chapter 2
# Significance

## THE WEIGHT OF YAHWEH'S NAME

When God called Moses to embark on the most important mission of his life, bringing the children of Israel out of Egyptian bondage, He equipped him with the power and authority of His mighty, matchless name, Yahweh! Moses, however, at first, had doubts that Israel even knew Him or His name.

*Then Moses replied to **Elohim**, "Suppose I go to the people of Israel and say to them, 'The **Elohim** of your ancestors has sent me to you,' and they ask me, 'What is his name?' What should I tell them?" **Elohim** answered Moses, "**Ehyeh** Who **Ehyeh**. This is what you must say to the people of Israel: '**Ehyeh** has sent me to you.'" Again **Elohim** said* *to Moses, "This is what you must say to the people of Israel: **Yahweh Elohim** of your ancestors, the **Elohim** of Abraham, Isaac, and Jacob, has sent me to you. This is my name forever. This is my title throughout every generation." (Exodus 3:13-15 NOG)*

The mighty name Yahweh is just as significant for us today. When we speak the name Yahweh, we become acutely aware of whom we are calling upon, rather than just casually or offhandedly saying God or LORD, a title sometimes said in haste with no thought of His majesty and power. Yahweh's name is great and worthy to be praised.

*Forasmuch as there is none like unto thee, O Yahweh; thou art great, and thy name is great in might. (Jeremiah 10:6 RSB)*

*Sing unto Elohim, sing praises to his name: extol him that rideth upon the heavens by his name YAH, and rejoice before him. (Psalm 68:4 RSB)*

*For great is Yahweh, and greatly to be praised: he also is to be feared above all mighty ones. (1 Chronicles 16:25 RSB)*

I challenge you to begin to purposefully and respectfully speak the names of Yahweh and Yahshua, rather than just stating the generic titles of LORD and God. As you call upon the mighty name of Yah, you will begin to comprehend the power and influence of His name, and you will actually think about and be sensitive to what you are saying. You won't want to use the names of Yahweh and Yahshua vainly, fruitlessly, or without meaning or purpose, as the terms God and LORD are sometimes used today.

You will soon go beyond calling on the transliterated name of Jesus; because the English name of Jesus is, sadly, often used blasphemously, idly, and as an expression of profanity. We need to begin calling upon the names of Yahweh and Yahshua, the original Hebrew names spoken by God Himself.

## THE TRUTH WILL MAKE YOU FREE

While some chase after a supernatural experience without a real commitment and some long for a "religious" experience, others yearn for a genuine relationship with the living God by abiding in the truth of His Word. When we have an intimate relationship with Yahweh, through belief in Yahshua, the Living Word, we are a vibrant testimony to God's goodness.

Through the risen Messiah, we are living a resurrected life in real time[2], and Yahshua becomes the living Torah, the living Word of Yahweh manifested in our lives and in our culture. People can see a genuine reflection of Yah through our submission to Him in our everyday lives, and the kingdom of heaven is brought to earth when we submit to and live in accordance with the truth of the Word of God.

> **Yahshua is the living Word of Yahweh.**

When deprived of the truth of Yahweh, cultures embrace false gods, idols, counterfeit religions, or deny

---

[2] Reverend Vern Shepherd; Lakeside United Methodist Church, Lakeside, Ohio; April 20, 2014

the very existence of God. Furthermore, when society blatantly refuses to embrace the truth of Yahweh and confess that Yahshua is the way, the truth, and the life, idolatry easily slithers into the culture; nevertheless, we are not without hope, for there is a promise attached to knowing the truth.

*And you shall know the truth, and the truth shall make you free. (John 8:32 ISR)*

*For this is good and acceptable in the sight of Elohim our Saviour; Who will have all men to be saved, and to come unto the knowledge of the truth. (1 Timothy 2:3-4 RSB)*

When we embrace the Word of God, our lives are positively impacted; on the other hand, when we don't embrace His Word, our lives are negatively impacted. It is imperative that we actively seek to know the truth, because ignorance does not cancel the truth.

*I will destroy my people because they are ignorant. You have refused to learn, so I will refuse to let you be my priests. You have forgotten the teachings of your **Elohim**, so I will forget your children. (Hosea 4:6 NOG)*

*My people have perished for lack of knowledge. Because you have rejected knowledge, I reject you from being priest for Me. Since you have forgotten the Torah of your Elohim, I also forget your children. (Hosea 4:6 ISR)*

Whether or not we know the truth doesn't change the truth. For instance, even if we don't know which foods are healthy or unhealthy, our bodies are impacted by our choices. When we eat the wrong foods, our bodies suffer. When we eat the right foods, our bodies flourish. In like manner, just as ingesting the wrong physical food affects the natural body, ingesting the wrong spiritual food affects the body of Christ.

We must study the Word of God, because it's only the truth we know that makes us free. Without the knowledge of the truth, we face dire consequences. Yahweh has commanded us to refrain from murder; and if someone commits murder, they will be punished. Even if they claim not to know that murder is a crime, it doesn't cancel the law against murder. The justice system rightly assumes that most people, with few exceptions, know that murdering another human being is wrong.

It's interesting to note that not all truth is accepted as truth. While society and the church agree murder and stealing are wrong, there is a gray area when it comes to Yahweh's instructions regarding idols, keeping the Sabbath, not taking His name in vain, not lying nor coveting, and not committing adultery. Even though the culture may see a gray area in some of Yahweh's instructions, believers in Yahweh have a higher standard and must strive to adhere to His teachings.

> **Not all truth is accepted as truth.**

When we reject the Word of God as truth, we become imprisoned and bound within the deception of the enemy, and we cannot be set free. By denying the truth of His Word, we are denying that Yahweh's instructions are actually valid and true.

Consequently, because we deny the truth, we neither recognize nor accept that some of the calamities in our lives are as a result of rejecting the Word of Yahweh; nevertheless, when we truly repent, change our mind, and embrace His Word as truth, the truth will make us free!

## YAHWEH'S INSTRUCTIONS ARE STILL VALID

Yahweh has given us specific instructions, so we can live a victorious life. When we ignore those instructions, there are consequences, whether we realize it or not. If you ignore the owner's manual for your car and fail to follow the instructions for regular maintenance, your car will eventually be rendered useless. Just because you have an owner's manual does not mean your car will, regardless of how you treat it, magically operate as it should. You must follow the instructions.

The same principle is true for Yahweh's instructions. He issued His Word out of His deep, abiding love for humanity. He knows unequivocally what is best for us, because He created us and the world we live in. If I, for example, continually reject Yahweh's Word, I will eventually suffer so many dire consequences for disobedience that I will become hopeless and confused, as I continue to deny the truth.

When Yahweh instituted the law of gravity, it was not to harm us. God created the law of gravity to keep us grounded on our planet, so that we would not fly off into space. When He commanded us not to murder, it was to protect us, not to hurt us. Whether we understand it or accept it, all of Yahweh's instructions are designed to protect us from lawlessness, chaos, and destruction.

We must realize that Yahweh's teachings about His name are just as important as any other instruction He has given. Even as Satan attacked Job with a steady barrage of demonically-inspired tragedies (the loss of his children, his health, and his wealth), Job recognized the importance of praising Yahweh's name.

*He (Job) said, "Naked I came from my mother, and naked I will return. **Yahweh** has given, and **Yahweh** has taken away! **May the name of Yahweh be praised**." (emphasis added) (Job 1:21 NOG)*

Job was declaring, even in his darkest hour, "May the authority (name) of Yahweh be praised!" Job did not doubt the sovereign authority of Yahweh over his life!

King David recognized the significance of calling on Yahweh. Throughout the 16th chapter of 1 Chronicles, David praises His name.

*When David had finished sacrificing burnt offerings and fellowship offerings, he blessed the people **in the name of Yahweh**. (emphasis added) (1 Chronicles 16:2 NOG)*

*"Give thanks to **Yahweh**. Call on his name. Make known among the nations what he has done." (1 Chronicles 16:8 NOG)*

*"Brag about his holy name. Let the hearts of those who seek **Yahweh** rejoice." (1 Chronicles 16:10 NOG)*

*"Give to **Yahweh**, you families of the nations. Give to **Yahweh** glory and power. Give to **Yahweh** the glory his name deserves. Bring an*

48

*offering, and come to him. Worship **Yahweh** in his holy splendor." (1 Chronicles 16:28-29 NOG)*

*"Give thanks to **Yahweh** because he is good, because his mercy endures forever. Say, 'Rescue us, O **Elohim** our Savior. Gather us and save us from the nations so that we may give thanks to your holy name and make your praise our glory.' Thanks be to **Yahweh Elohim** of Israel from everlasting to everlasting." (1 Chronicles 16:34-36a NOG)*

When we assemble together as a body of believers, we should lift up the precious name of Yahweh. If we do not lift up His holy name in our assemblies, it's like having a celebration or a festive party and never acknowledging and honoring the invited guest.

*Praise **Yahweh's** greatness with me. Let us highly honor his name together. (Psalm 34:3 NOG)*

*O magnify Yahweh with me, and let us exalt his name together. (Psalm 34:3 RSB)*

As we praise Yahweh, He inhabits our praise. Calling on and lifting up His name in praise invites Him to dwell with us and in us.

> **Yahweh inhabits our praise.**

*But thou art holy, O thou that inhabitest the praises of Israel. (Psalm 22:3 RSB)*

## HASHEM

I believe Yahweh's name has significance and deep meaning and that His name must be praised and highly exalted, but there are those who feel His name is inexpressible, unpronounceable, or ineffable (should not be pronounced), so they call Him HaShem, which in Hebrew literally means The Name. Yahweh's name, however, is a reflection of His eternal authority and power: "He is now and forever will be who He is and will be." There is no other god in the universe for whom that statement of fact is true.

People worship gods of weather, gods of fortune, gods of calamity, gods created by the human imagination and fashioned by human hands, gods that are definitely not eternal nor self-existent. Yahweh is now and will forever be the one and only true God who spoke the universe into being and yet is concerned for the welfare of His people. Yahweh's name, therefore, cannot be replaced by the term HaShem.

HaShem is not His name, and it does not describe Yahweh at all. Yahweh is His name forever, according to Exodus 3:15 (NOG).

*Again **Elohim** said to Moses, "This is what you must say to the people of Israel: **Yahweh Elohim** of your ancestors, the **Elohim** of Abraham, Isaac, and Jacob, has sent me to you. This is my name forever. This is my title throughout every generation."*

Yahweh did not instruct us to call Him "The Name" forever. He proclaimed Yahweh to be His name and Elohim to be His title forever! The term "HaShem" doesn't reflect even one of Yahweh's unique attributes. For instance, El Shaddai means God Almighty. El Elyon means God Most High. Yahweh Melech is Yahweh King. El Ruach is God's Spirit. Yahweh Elohim is Yahweh God. Yahweh Adonai is Yahweh Lord. The list goes on and on. Every title of God in Hebrew has a significant meaning and describes an aspect of His eternal nature when translated to English, but "The Name" fails to describe even one attribute of the eternal God who is all-powerful, all-knowing, and ever present. Those who believe Yahweh's name should never be spoken are following a principle that was instituted centuries ago by religious leaders who built fences around Yahweh's instruction regarding His name and forbade the utterance of His name, because they wanted to ensure that God's name would never be dishonored, profaned, or blasphemed.

Some feel unworthy to speak the name Yahweh, believing His name is unutterable and shouldn't be spoken under any circumstances. At times, it seems as though they are even offended at the mention of His name and become very defensive. In a zealous attempt to never take Yahweh's name in vain (by speaking HaShem as an alternate or replacement), Yahweh's name is actually being blotted out and obliterated from memory. Genesis 4:26 would make no sense if translated literally using the name HaShem in place of the LORD. *King James* translates it this way:

*And to Seth, to him also there was born a son; and he called his name Enos: then began men to call upon the name of the LORD.*

Translated using HaShem would render the verse:

*And to Seth, to him also there was born a son; and he called his name Enos: then began men to call upon the name of The Name.*

Genesis 12:8 as rendered in the *King James* translation:

*And he removed from thence unto a mountain on the east of Bethel, and pitched his tent, having Bethel on the west, and Hai on the east: and there he builded an altar unto the LORD, and called upon the name of the LORD.*

Translated using HaShem:

*And he removed from thence unto a mountain on the east of Bethel, and pitched his tent, having Bethel on the west, and Hai on the east: and there he builded an altar unto the Name, and called upon the name of The Name.*

Yahweh reveals, through the prophet Joel, that there is an eternal reward for those who call on His name.

*"I will work miracles in the sky and on the earth: blood, fire, and clouds of smoke. The sun will become dark, and the moon will become as red as blood before the terrifying day of **Yahweh** comes." Then whoever calls on the name of **Yahweh** will be saved. Those who escape will be on Mount Zion and in Jerusalem. Among the survivors will be those whom **Yahweh** calls, as **Yahweh** has promised. (Joel 2:30-32 NOG)*

Translated using HaShem, The Name:

*"I will work miracles in the sky and on the earth: blood, fire, and clouds of smoke. The sun will become dark, and the moon will become as red as blood before the terrifying day of The Name comes." Then whoever calls on the name of The Name will be saved. Those who escape will be on Mount Zion and in Jerusalem. Among the survivors will be those whom The Name calls, as The Name has promised.*

Which of these versions gives honor to Yahweh? Which passage makes it clear upon whom we should call to be saved? Who will be saved? Those who call on the name of The Name, or those who call on the name of Yahweh? There are many verses that read, "call on the name of Yahweh," where substituting "the name of The Name" just doesn't make it clear that we are calling upon Yahweh.

I respectfully submit that one should not substitute Yahweh's name with the title "The Name," nor should His name be blotted out and ignored. Yahweh is not an anonymous God, and His personal name cannot be reduced to the very general term "HaShem."

Although the term "HaShem" shows respect for the name of Yahweh, "HaShem" does not sufficiently describe the singularly unique nature of Yahweh; therefore, even though "HaShem" can be used to show reverence for the divine name, it should not be used to replace the name Yahweh. Yahweh is very unique, and His name is unique, as well. We should not

**Yahweh is unique.**

refer to Him only in generic terms, such as LORD, God, or The Name. He is LORD and God, but those are only titles and should not replace the actual name Yahweh. His titles are only significant when we realize and express the relationship of His titles to His name. We must call Yahweh by His matchless name, and take special care to call upon His name reverently. We must not trivialize His name by speaking it profanely, blasphemously, frivolously, nor by habitually repeating His name with no purpose.

Even though I don't agree with those who choose to suppress Yahweh's name, I do respect the reverence they give His name, and it makes me very careful how and when I speak His name. I am ever mindful not to misspeak when I utter the name Yahweh. I understand the reasoning for not wanting to say His name, but God did not command us to blot out His name nor to censor His name.

Yahshua did not die to separate us from Yahweh; Yahshua sacrificed His life so that we could experience a personal relationship with God and be one with Him. Speaking the name of Yahweh, in my opinion, is a way to experience and cultivate that relationship. On the other hand, by replacing Yahweh's name with a vague generic term, we unwittingly put up a spiritual wall of separation that Yahshua died to destroy.

I mentioned in the previous chapter that korban is the Hebrew word meaning "draw near to God with an offering." The offerings brought by Israel in the Old Testament were offerings for sin, trespass, atonement, goodwill, and peace. Yahshua is the embodiment of every one of these offerings.

*In this passage Christ first said, "You did not want sacrifices, offerings, burnt offerings, and sacrifices for sin. You did not approve of them." (These are the sacrifices that Moses' Teachings require people to offer.) Then Christ says, "I have come to do what you want." He did away with sacrifices in order to establish the obedience that God wants. We have been set apart as holy because **Yeshua** Christ did what God wanted him to do by sacrificing his body once and for all. Every day each priest performed his religious duty. He offered the same type of sacrifice again and again. Yet, these sacrifices could never take away sins. However, this chief priest made one sacrifice for sins, and this sacrifice lasts forever. Then he received the highest position in heaven. Since that time, he has been waiting for his enemies to be made his footstool. With one sacrifice he accomplished the work of setting them apart for God forever. (Hebrews 10:8-14 NOG)*

Yahshua is not only our Passover Lamb that atones for our sin. He is our High Priest forever! This truly is good news that the very One who died for us has authority over us. He knows what we face each and every day, and He gives us the power to overcome every obstacle through the power of the Holy Spirit.

Yes, there are dire consequences for blaspheming Yahweh's name; but we should not live in such fear of manmade rules that we refuse to speak His name at all and then do everything we can to keep His name a secret. Yahweh's name is glorious and should be exalted! Yahshua has given us entry into the holy place, and we can call upon His glorious name in worship and love.

It's a fact that some people speak the name of Jesus in an evil and profane way. Yet, we, as believers, do not refuse to speak His name. We don't let the fear that we will misuse Jesus' name or that others will misuse it in a profane or vulgar way keep us from speaking His wonderful name. In the same way, we must not let the enemy strike such fear in us that we are afraid to even mention the name Yahweh.

*For Elohim hath not given us the spirit of fear; but of power, and of love, and of a sound mind. (2 Timothy 1:7 RSB)*

# יהוה
## צבאות

# Chapter 3
# Authority

## THE AUTHORITY OF A NAME AND TITLE

What is the appropriate protocol for addressing someone in authority? Do we address them by their name only, or by their name and title? Does the protocol change for different settings and in different relationships? If you have a close relationship with someone who holds a position of authority, should you address them by name only, by title only, or by name and title?

For example, if someone holds the position of governor of a state, those who address the governor may sometimes use only his title and at other times they may use the governor's name and title.

Let's use another example. Say, for instance, at your place of employment a man introduces himself as Mr.

John Jones, the Chief Executive Officer; furthermore, he makes it clear that he prefers to be addressed as Mr. Jones. For someone to then greet Mr Jones by saying, "Hello, Chief Executive Officer," every time they speak to him, would be disrespectful and would go against the specific instructions and wishes of Mr. Jones.

Just as our names and titles distinguish us and set us apart from one another, Yahweh's very distinct name and titles distinguish Him and set Him apart from all other gods and idols. False gods do not have the unique, holy attributes of Yahweh, such as love, compassion, mercy, kindness, truth, goodness, justice, honesty, integrity, honor, virtue, righteousness, purity, holiness, perfection, generosity, sovereignty, omniscience (all knowledge), omnipotence (all-powerful), omnipresence (in all places), and much, much more.

Yahweh's name truly describes Him as boundless, limitless, immeasurable, and eternal: "He is now and forever will be who He is and will be."

## YAHWEH CALLS US BY NAME

Our names are meaningful, and they set us apart from one another; therefore, it should not be surprising to know that Yahweh calls us by name.

*But now thus saith Yahweh that created thee, O Jacob, and he that formed thee, O Israel, Fear not: for I have redeemed thee, I have called thee by thy name; thou art mine. (Isaiah 43:1 RSB)*

*But now, thus said* יהוה *(Yahweh), your Creator, O Ya'aqob, and He who formed you, O Yisra'ĕl, "Do not fear, for I have redeemed you. I have called you by your name, you are Mine." (Isaiah 43:1 ISR)*

*"He who overcomes shall be dressed in white robes, and I shall by no means blot out his name from the Book of Life, but I shall confess his name before My Father and before His messengers." (Revelation 3:5 ISR)*

***Yahweh** answered Moses, "I will do what you have asked, because I am pleased with you, and I know you by name." (Exodus 33:17 NOG)*

How beautiful it is to realize that Yahweh knows us and calls us by name. We are created in God's image; therefore, if He considered it important enough to call us by name, we should consider it important enough to call Him by name. What an amazing love He radiates toward us, and it doesn't end there. Additionally, Yahweh blesses us tremendously when we call Him by name.

***Yahweh** said to Moses, "Tell Aaron and his sons, 'This is how you will bless the Israelites. Say to them: **Yahweh** will bless you and watch over you. **Yahweh** will smile on you and be kind to you. **Yahweh** will look on you with favor and give you peace.' So whenever they use my name to bless the Israelites, I will bless them." (Numbers 6:22-27 NOG)*

*Because you love me, I will rescue you. I will protect you because you know my name. (Psalm 91:14 NOG)*

*Turn toward me, and have pity on me as you have pledged to do for those who love your name. (Psalm 119:132 NOG)*

*"Since you were precious in My eyes, you have been esteemed, and I have loved you. And I give men in your place, and peoples for your life. Do not fear, for I am with you. I shall bring your seed from the east, and gather you from the west. I shall say to the north, 'Give them up!' And to the south, 'Do not keep them back!' Bring My sons from afar, and My daughters from the ends of the earth – all those who are called by My Name, whom I have created, formed, even made for My esteem." (Isaiah 43:4-7 ISR)*

*And יהוה (Yahweh) is a refuge for the crushed one, A refuge in times of distress. And those who know Your Name trust in You, For You have not forsaken those who seek You, O יהוה (Psalm 9:9-10 ISR)*

*And it shall be that everyone who calls on the name of יהוה shall be delivered. For on Mount Tsiyon and in Yerushalayim there shall be an escape as יהוה has said, and among the survivors whom יהוה calls. (Joel 2:32 ISR)*

*'And it shall be that everyone who calls on the Name of יהוה shall be saved.' (Acts 2:21 ISR)*

Salvation, deliverance, and power are the rewards for all who execute the authority of the name of Yahweh, but the authority of His name has no power if His name is not spoken.

The entire universe was created by God's spoken Word. In the very first chapter of Genesis, it says repeatedly, "God said..." As a result of God's spoken Word, light and darkness, heaven and earth, the seas, grass, herbs, trees, the moon, sun, stars, animals, birds, fish, cattle, creeping things, man, woman, and all things that exist were created. Believers, by invoking the authority of Yahweh, in Yahshua's name, have power to create miracles.

> **The entire universe was created by God's Word.**

*I will do anything you ask the Father in my name so that the Father will be given glory because of the Son. (John 14:13 NOG)*

*If ye shall ask any thing in my name, I will do it. (John 14:14 RSB)*

*But the Comforter, which is the Holy Spirit, whom the Father will send in my name, he shall teach you all things, and bring all things to your remembrance, whatsoever I have said unto you. (John 14:26 RSB)*

*Ye have not chosen me, but I have chosen you, and ordained you, that ye should go and bring forth fruit, and that your fruit should remain: that whatsoever ye shall ask of the Father in my name, he may give it you. (John 15:16 RSB)*

*And in that day ye shall ask me nothing. Verily, verily, I say unto you, Whatsoever ye shall ask the Father in my name, he will give it you. Hitherto have ye asked nothing in my name: ask, and ye shall receive, that your joy may be full. (John 16:23-24 RSB)*

*At that day ye shall ask in my name: and I say not unto you, that I will pray the Father for you: For the Father himself loveth you, because ye have loved me, and have believed that I came out from Elohim. (John 16:26-27 RSB)*

We must not hide the name of Yahweh nor the name of Yahshua, for there is power and authority in the name of Yah!

## AUTHORITY WITHIN THE FAMILY

There is a set order of authority and therefore power within the family unit. The various levels of authority are recognized within the titles given to each family member, such as dad, mom, sons, daughters, uncles, aunts, and cousins, to name a few. In relation to underage children, Dad and Mom are the highest authority in the family; uncles and aunts come next in authority; and sons and daughters have a different level of authority.

To distinguish each family member even further, specific names are used. For example, when introducing your mom or dad to someone, you would say, "This is my mom," or "This is my dad," and you would mention their proper name, because the person you're introducing them to would most likely not call them just Mom or Dad.

Furthermore, if your dad holds a position of authority within an organization, and you have the task of introducing him to an employee or group of employees, you would introduce him by both his name and title, such as, "Mr. John Jones, Chief Executive Officer."

You wouldn't introduce him just as your dad. He deserves the utmost respect of having his position and authority made known to those who are serving him as employees, even though he is your dad.

Several years ago, I regularly attended a mega church of about 5,000 members. The pastor of the church is a prominent, well-known minister of the Gospel, a best-selling author, and he hosts a worldwide television program broadcast on hundreds of major Christian and secular television stations.

The pastor's daughter often introduces him at ministry events, and she always respectfully introduces him by name and title, even though he is her dad. If she should mention to a congregation that he is her dad, as she sometimes does, she still gives him the honor and respect due his position of authority. She submits to his authority as her dad and as her pastor, introducing him by name and title; consequently, since she submits to and honors his authority, God promises to give her a long life filled with blessing.

*"Respect your father and your mother, so that your days are prolonged upon the soil which* יהוה *your Elohim is giving you." (Exodus 20:12 ISR)*

*"Children, obey your parents in the Master, for this is right. 'Respect your father and mother,' which is the first command with promise, in order that it might be well with you, and you might live long on the earth." (Ephesians 6:1-3 ISR)*

## ABBA (DADDY) YAHWEH

Just as the pastor's daughter just spoken of honors the position and authority of her dad, we must honor Yahweh, our Abba, Father, and Daddy. Even though He is Daddy, we must still respect and reverence His position of authority by calling Him by name, when appropriate, especially when speaking of Him to others. People must know our Father by name and title, that He is Yahweh, God Almighty, El Shaddai.

We must give our heavenly Father the respect He deserves. He is the Creator of the universe, and we call Him Creator; He is our Savior, and we call Him Savior; He is our Father, and we call Him Father; and He is also Yahweh, the Eternal Almighty King who deserves the utmost respect.

As explained previously, there are many false gods in the world, gods made by human hands and invented by human imagination. When I say "God," people need to know to whom I am referring. I need to use His name to set Him apart from all the other gods, especially if I'm speaking to someone of a different faith background who may worship a different god or gods.

*Give thanks to* **Yahweh**. *Call on him. Make known among the nations what he has done. (Psalm 105:1 NOG)*

*Praise Yah! Praise O servants of* יהוה. *Praise the Name of* יהוה*! Blessed be the Name of* יהוה*, now and forever! From the rising of the sun to its going down, the Name of* יהוה *is praised ... Praise Yah! (Psalm 113:1-3,9b ISR)*

*And let them know that You, Whose Name is* יהוה
*You alone are the Most High over all the earth.*
*(Psalm 83:18 ISR)*

Yahweh is bringing His name out of hiding and making it known again to His enemies and, most importantly, making His name, position, and authority known again to His people.

*If only you would split open the heavens and come down! The mountains would quake at your presence. Be like the fire that kindles brushwood and makes water boil. Come down to make your name known to your enemies. The nations will tremble in your presence. (Isaiah 64:1-2 NOG)*

*No one calls on your name or tries to hold on to you. You have hidden your face from us. You have let us be ruined by our sins. But now,* **Yahweh,** *you are our* **Ab (Father).** *We are the clay, and you are our potter. We are the work of your hands. (Isaiah 64:7-8 NOG)*

*"He who has an ear, let him hear what the Spirit says to the assemblies. To him who overcomes I shall give some of the hidden manna to eat. And I shall give him a white stone, and on the stone a renewed Name written which no one knows except him who receives it." (Revelation 2:17 ISR)*

*He who overcomes, I shall make him a supporting post in the Dwelling Place of My Elohim, and he shall by no means go out. And I shall write on him the Name of My Elohim and the name of the city of My Elohim, the renewed Yerushalayim, which*

*comes down out of the heaven from My Elohim,
and My renewed Name. (Revelation 3:12 ISR)*

## YAHWEH IN YAHSHUA

There are many, many Scripture verses that
instruct us to exalt Yahweh's name, praise His name,
glorify His name, and receive power and authority in
His name. Because of the immeasurable value of
knowing and proclaiming Yahweh's name, I believe His
name has been restored in the name of Yahshua, God
the Son.

*I am come in my Father's name... (John 5:43a
KJV)*

The religious leaders in Yahshua's day recognized
that Yahshua spoke in the authority of Yahweh and
that Yahshua performed mighty works in His Father's
name. The Pharisees were so threatened by Yahshua's
authority that they wanted to stone Him.

> **Yeshua** *told them, "If God were your Father, you
> would love me ... The person who belongs to God
> understands what God says. You don't
> understand because you don't belong to God ...
> Your father Abraham was pleased to see that my
> day was coming. He saw it and was happy." The
> Jews said to* **Yeshua,** *"You're not even fifty years
> old. How could you have seen Abraham?"* **Yeshua**
> *told them, "I can guarantee this truth: Before
> Abraham was ever born, I am." Then some of the
> Jews picked up stones to throw at* **Yeshua.**
> *However,* **Yeshua** *was concealed, and he left the
> temple courtyard. (John 8:42a,47,56-59 NOG)*

When Yahshua said, "I AM," the religious leaders knew what He was saying. He was telling them He was eternal, and there is only One who can make that claim: Yahweh. If there is any doubt that

> **Yahshua declared,
> "I AM!"**

Yahshua claimed to be God, consider this next passage.

> *Yeshua replied to them, "I've shown you many good things that come from the Father. For which of these good things do you want to stone me to death?" The Jews answered Yeshua, "We're going to stone you to death, not for any good things you've done, but for dishonoring God. You claim to be God, although you're only a man." (John 10:32-33 NOG)*

The religious leaders told Yahshua, "You claim to be God, but you are only a man." They just could not accept that Yahweh could manifest Himself in any way He desired, and especially not in human form. They put Yahweh in a box, and they were not going to let Him out. Yahshua, however, was not intimidated by the religious leaders, and He would go on to announce His identity many times. Yahshua did not try to hide. He knew He was on a collision course with His opponents, and He was about to meet the adversary head-on.

## THE "I AM" DECLARATIONS OF YAHSHUA

Following is a list of the "I AM" declarations of Yahshua. It is my suggestion that you read them carefully and meditate on each one of them, letting each word sink into your spirit, knowing Yahshua is

Yahweh. Do not just look them over quickly. Let the Holy Spirit minister to you, as you contemplate the fullness of Yahweh in Yahshua.

*And Yahshua said unto them, I am the bread of life: he that cometh to me shall never hunger; and he that believeth on me shall never thirst. (John 6:35 RSB)*

*Then spake Yahshua again unto them, saying, I am the light of the world: he that followeth me shall not walk in darkness, but shall have the light of life. (John 8:12 RSB)*

*Then said Yahshua unto them again, Verily, verily, I say unto you, I am the door of the sheep. All that ever came before me are thieves and robbers: but the sheep did not hear them. I am the door: by me if any man enter in, he shall be saved, and shall go in and out, and find pasture. (John 10:7-9 RSB)*

*I am the good shepherd: the good shepherd giveth his life for the sheep. But he that is an hireling, and not the shepherd, whose own the sheep are not, seeth the wolf coming, and leaveth the sheep, and fleeth: and the wolf catcheth them, and scattereth the sheep. The hireling fleeth, because he is an hireling, and careth not for the sheep. I am the good shepherd, and know my sheep, and am known of mine. (John 10:11-14 RSB)*

*Yahshua said unto her, I am the resurrection, and the life: he that believeth in me, though he were dead yet shall he live: (John 11:25 RSB)*

*Yahshua saith unto him, I am the way, the truth, and the life: no man cometh unto the Father, but by me. (John 14:6 RSB)*

*I am the true vine, and my Father is the husbandman. Every branch in me that beareth not fruit he taketh away: and every branch that beareth fruit, he purgeth it, that it may bring forth more fruit. Now ye are clean through the word which I have spoken unto you. Abide in me, and I in you. As the branch cannot bear fruit of itself, except it abide in the vine; no more can ye, except ye abide in me. I am the vine, ye are the branches: He that abideth in me, and I in him, the same bringeth forth much fruit: for without me ye can do nothing. (John 15:1-5 RSB)*

Just by the simple claim, "I AM (EHYEH)," in each of the preceding verses, Yahshua is declaring He is Yahweh. Remember, when God says, "EHYEH ASHER EHYEH," He is the only one who can describe Himself in that way. Yahshua proclaims, "I AM AND WILL BE" the Bread of life, the Light of the world, the Door, the Good Shepherd, the Resurrection, the Way, the Truth, the Life, and the True Vine. When we speak the name Yah, we proclaim, "HE IS!" (EHYEH means I AM; YAHWEH means HE IS.)

Yahshua's deity is also confirmed in the following verses by two Gospel writers, Matthew and Luke.

*The Son of man shall send forth his angels, and they shall gather out of his kingdom all things that offend, and them which do iniquity; (Matthew 13:41 RSB)*

*Also I say unto you, Whosoever shall confess me before men, him shall the Son of man also confess before the angels of God: But he that denieth me before men shall be denied before the angels of God. (Luke 12:8-9 KJV)*

Matthew makes it clear that the angels and Kingdom mentioned in the first verse belong to Yahshua; and then Luke, in the second verse, makes it clear that the angels belong to God. Here, again, Scripture confirms Yahshua's deity. In the Father, Son, and Holy Spirit, Yahweh is one God fulfilling three roles. The Creator entered His creation to fulfill His plan and purpose of redemption and bring His Kingdom to earth. Yahshua instructed His disciples to pray:

*Let your kingdom come. Let your will be done on earth as it is done in heaven. (Matthew 6:10 NOG)*

As time began to draw to a close on Yahshua's earthly ministry, He encouraged His disciples with these words:

*I will ask the Father, and he will give you another helper who will be with you forever. That helper is the Spirit of Truth. The world cannot accept him, because it doesn't see or know him. You know him, because he lives with you and will be in you. (John 14:16-17 NOG)*

The preceding verse describes the third role Yah plays in the believer. He is not locked out of His creation. He gave His life as a ransom for His people and gives His Spirit to help us walk in truth and power. By the power of His Spirit, He dwells within us. It brings to mind His words to Moses: "I am and will forever be with you," which is the very definition of His name.

> **Yah is not locked out of His creation.**

There are many verses throughout Scripture that give us clues, some subtle and some not so subtle, about the manifestation of God in the flesh, Yahweh in Yahshua. Here are a few verses for your consideration.

*And I will pour upon the house of David, and upon the inhabitants of Jerusalem, the spirit of grace and of supplications: and they shall look upon me whom they have pierced, and they shall mourn for him, as one mourneth for his only son, and shall be in bitterness for him, as one that is in bitterness for his firstborn. (Zechariah 12:10 RSB)*

*Because I will publish the name of Yahweh: ascribe ye greatness unto our Elohim. He is the Rock, his work is perfect: for all his ways are judgment: an El of truth and without iniquity, just and right is he. (Deuteronomy 32:3-4 RSB)*

*O come, let us sing unto Yahweh: let us make a joyful noise to the rock of our salvation (Yahshua). (Psalm 95:1 RSB)*

*Moreover, brethren, I would not that ye should be ignorant, how that all our fathers were under the cloud, and all passed through the sea; And were all baptized unto Moses in the cloud and in the sea; And did all eat the same spiritual meat; And did all drink the same spiritual drink: for they drank of that spiritual Rock that followed them: and that Rock was Messiah. (1 Corinthians 10:1-4 RSB)*

*Pay attention to yourselves and to the entire flock in which the Holy Spirit has placed you as bishops to be shepherds for God's church which he acquired with his own blood. (Acts 20:28 NOG)*

*Be careful not to let anyone rob you of this faith through a shallow and misleading philosophy. Such a person follows human traditions and the world's way of doing things rather than following Christ. All of God lives in Christ's body, and God has made you complete in Christ. Christ is in charge of every ruler and authority. (Colossians 2:8-10 NOG)*

*God has rescued us from the power of darkness and has brought us into the kingdom of his Son, whom he loves. His Son paid the price to free us, which means that our sins are forgiven. He is the image of the invisible God, the firstborn of all creation. He created all things in heaven and on earth, visible and invisible. Whether they are kings or lords, rulers or powers—everything has been created through him and for him. He existed before everything and holds everything together. He is also the head of the church, which is his body. He is the beginning, the first to come back to life so that he would have first place in everything. God was pleased to have all of himself live in Christ. God was also pleased to bring everything on earth and in heaven back to himself through Christ. He did this by making peace through Christ's blood sacrificed on the cross. (Colossians 1:13-20 NOG)*

*The mystery that gives us our reverence for God is acknowledged to be great: He appeared in his human nature, was approved by the Spirit, was seen by angels, was announced throughout the nations, was believed in the world, and was taken to heaven in glory. (1 Timothy 3:16 NOG)*

To the unbeliever, it's incredulous to think that God can manifest Himself in three ways, but for the believer it's not hard to fathom it at all. He is God Almighty, El Shaddai, and He can manifest Himself in any way He desires for the purpose of redeeming His people. Refusing to believe that Yahshua and Yahweh are one is denying the power and sovereignty of Yah. If we put Him in a box to serve our own selfish purposes and fit the mold we want Him to fit, we are not fully believing in Him and His divine power. Yahshua Himself said nothing is impossible for God, and with God all things are possible.

**With God all things are possible.**

*He (Yahshua) told them (the disciples), "Because you have so little faith (speaking of their failure to cast a demon out of a boy referenced in*

*Matthew 17:19). I can guarantee this truth: If your faith is the size of a mustard seed, you can say to this mountain, 'Move from here to there,' and it will move. Nothing will be impossible for you." (Matthew 17:20 NOG)*

*But Yahshua beheld them, and said unto them, With men this is impossible; but with Yahweh all things are possible. (Matthew 19:26 RSB)*

Yah is not limited by our limited spiritual vision. Yahshua came to regain possession of the Father's beloved children from the enemy of our souls. Yahshua's sacrifice has restored us to a right relationship with Yahweh and exposed the enemy. Part of the enemy's plan is to keep Yahweh's name hidden. Knowing God's name creates an intimate relationship with our Creator that frees us from the misconception that Yah is a distant, merciless God who cares nothing about our plight.

The adversary does not want humanity to know God by His personal name. He wants to keep us from knowing God as a very personal Father who sent His only begotten Son on a mission to rescue and redeem mankind. The enemy wants to block us from having an intimate relationship with our Creator. Just as his mission was to drive Adam and Eve from the Garden, his mission is to keep us separated from Yahweh and prevent us from being returned back to the original state and purpose for which we were created: to have a loving relationship with Yah.

There should be neither shame nor fear in speaking the name of God. Yes, we should fear Yahweh and fear missing the mark and falling short, but speaking His name is not something we should fear. Speaking His beautiful, incredible, wonderful name is a gift we should cherish and fully appreciate. We should be very grateful that the God of the universe would consider us worthy enough to receive the revelation of His name thousands of times throughout His Word.

We must be spiritually mature and responsible enough to reverently speak the magnificent names of Yahweh and Yahshua. We will then reap incredible blessings as we walk in the power and authority of the name of Yah, for there is salvation, deliverance, healing, power, righteousness, sanctification, freedom, prosperity, security, and victory in His name!

Yahweh controls everything and never fails. By the power of His spoken Word, He has created all things and set the entire universe in order. Let's use the authority and power of Yah's name to infuse His glorious kingdom and authority into our everyday reality; for Yahweh is concerned about every facet of our lives and is always present, ready, willing, and able to give us victory by shining His glorious light into our dark world. So, call on the name of Yahweh, in the name of Yahshua, and receive power from on high!

# Chapter 4
# Power

## THERE IS POWER IN HIS NAME

There truly is power in the names of Yahweh and Yahshua. In the name of Yah, we are victorious over sin and death. Because Yah is eternal, we have victory today and forever. The power we have in God's name does not increase nor diminish by speaking one name or the other. Yahweh and Yahshua are one. Notice how the following verses describe both Yahweh and Yahshua, proving they are One. Remember, Yahweh will not give His glory to another. Yah alone is:

## Savior:

*For I am Yahweh thy Elohim, the Holy One of Israel, thy Saviour... (Isaiah 43:3a RSB)*

*I, even I, am Yahweh; and beside me there is no saviour. (Isaiah 43:11 RSB)*

*I, **Yahweh**, speak what is fair and say what is right ... There is no other **Elohim** except me. There is no other righteous God and Savior besides me. Turn to me and be saved, all who live at the ends of the earth, because I am **El**, and there is no other. (Isaiah 45:19b,21b-22 NOG)*

*...and all flesh shall know that I Yahweh am thy Saviour and thy Redeemer, the mighty one of Jacob. (Isaiah 49:26b RSB)*

*For unto you is born this day in the city of David a Saviour, which is Messiah the Sovereign. (Luke 2:11 RSB)*

*And said unto the woman, Now we believe, not because of thy saying: for we have heard him ourselves, and know that this is indeed the Messiah, the Saviour of the world. (John 4:42 RSB)*

*Him hath Yahweh exalted with his right hand to be a Prince and a Saviour, for to give repentance to Israel, and forgiveness of sins. (Acts 5:31 RSB)*

*And we have seen and do testify that the Father sent the Son to be the Saviour of the world. (1 John 4:14 RSB)*

## The First and Last:

*Thus saith Yahweh the King of Israel, and his redeemer Yahweh of hosts; I am the first, and I am the last; and beside me there is no Elohim. (Isaiah 44:6 RSB)*

*And he said unto me, It is done. I am Alpha and Omega, the beginning and the end. I will give unto him that is athirst of the fountain of the water of life freely. (Revelation 21:6 RSB)*

*I am Alpha and Omega, the beginning and the end, the first and the last. (Revelation 22:13 RSB)*

## Faithful:

*For I am Yahweh, I change not; therefore ye sons of Jacob are not consumed. (Malachi 3:6 RSB)*

*Yahshua Messiah the same yesterday, and to day, and for ever. (Hebrews 13:8 RSB)*

## Shepherd:

*Yahweh is my shepherd; I shall not want. (Psalm 23:1 RSB)*

*Give ear, O Shepherd of Israel, thou that leadest Joseph like a flock; thou that dwellest between the cherubims, shine forth. (Psalm 80:1 RSB)*

*I (Yahshua) am the good shepherd: the good shepherd giveth his life for the sheep. (John 10:11 RSB)*

*I (Yahshua) am the good shepherd, and know my sheep, and am known of mine. (John 10:14 RSB)*

*And other sheep I have, which are not of this fold: them also I must bring, and they shall hear my voice; and there shall be one fold, and one shepherd. (John 10:16 RSB)*

*You were like lost sheep. Now you have come back to the shepherd and bishop of your lives. (1 Peter 2:25 NOG)*

*Then when the chief shepherd appears, you will receive the crown of glory that will never fade away. (1 Peter 5:4 NOG)*

## Supreme Final Authority:

*I have bound myself with an oath. A word has gone out from my righteous mouth that will not be recalled, "Every knee will bow to me and every tongue will swear allegiance." It will be said of me, "Certainly, righteousness and strength are found in* **Yahweh** *alone." (Isaiah 45:23-24a NOG)*

*Have the same attitude that Christ* **Yeshua** *had. Although he was in the form of God and equal with God, he did not take advantage of this equality. Instead, he emptied himself by taking on the form of a servant, by becoming like other humans, by having a human appearance. He humbled himself by becoming obedient to the point of death, death on a cross. This is why God has given him an exceptional honor—the name honored above all other names—so that at the name of* **Yeshua** *everyone in heaven, on earth, and in the world below will kneel and confess that*

*Yeshua Christ is Lord to the glory of God the Father. (Philippians 2:5-11 NOG)*

Note that in the phrase, "...confess that Yahshua Christ is Lord" in the preceding verse, the word Lord is the Greek word Kurios. As mentioned in a previous chapter, the Greek word Kurios represents the divine name Yahweh in the Septuagint, which is the Greek translation of the Old Testament. So this verse is actually saying, "...confess that Yahshua Messiah is Yahweh," which lines up harmoniously with Isaiah 45:23-24a.

In the Aramaic English New Testament (AENT), it states unequivocally in Philippians 2:10-11:

*...that at the name of Y'shua every knee should bow, of (beings) in heaven and on earth and under the earth; and that every tongue should confess that Master YHWH is Y'shua Mashiyach to the glory of Elohim his Father.*

All these verses highlight that Yahweh and Yahshua are One; therefore, whether we call upon the name of Yahweh or Yahshua, we are calling upon the Almighty God! When we call upon the name of Yah, we are calling upon the power and authority of His name! There is no one above Him. He is the Supreme Authority over all, and His name certainly reflects that fact.

Yahweh our God is eternal, and He is not a separate God or entity from Yahshua. He has no beginning and no end. As stated before, the very definition of His name proclaims, "He is now and forever will be who He is and will be," whether our Savior, Shepherd, Deliverer, or Supreme Authority. Yahweh did not send Yahshua as

His agent to rescue His people. He came in the flesh as Yahshua and rescued us Himself.

Even though Yahweh did have agents, prophets, and deliverers to help bring temporary rescue for His people in the Old Testament, the New Testament is about His divine act to come and rescue and save His people now and for all eternity. In the Old Testament, there was not one agent of Yahweh who could eternally rescue and deliver His people. Yahweh used different men and women multiple times to rescue and deliver Israel from one situation or another, one bondage or another, but there was not one who could secure their eternal salvation until Yahweh Himself came in the flesh as Yahshua. He gave His life to rescue us, if we would just confess Him as Savior and LORD (Yahweh).

> **Yahweh rescues and saves!**

Note that even though men and women were commissioned by God to help lead His people, the ultimate praise and glory belonged to Yahweh alone for their rescue, not to those who were commissioned.

In the book of Exodus, we see that even though Yahweh chose Moses to carry the authority and power of His name to Pharaoh, Pharaoh refused to recognize the sovereignty and dominion of Yahweh. So, Yahweh sent plagues upon Egypt to show His mighty power. Still, Pharaoh refused to submit to God's authority. Even as Yahweh sent plague after plague upon Egypt, showing Pharaoh who was in control, Pharaoh would not release the Israelites from slavery.

Just before the seventh plague (hail), Yahweh sent Moses yet again with a message for Pharaoh. Yahweh wanted Pharaoh to know the power and authority of His name.

*And for this reason I have raised you (Pharaoh) up, in order to show you My power, and in order to declare My Name in all the earth. (Exodus 9:16 ISR)*

It's absolutely astounding to know that one of the reasons God raised up Pharaoh was so that His name, Yahweh, would be declared in all the earth. He was letting Pharaoh and the world know that the only power Pharaoh had was the power given to him by Yahweh. After the tenth plague, the death of the firstborn, Pharaoh finally relented and released Israel from bondage, but even then he changed his mind, chased after them, and cornered them at the Red Sea. Yahweh then displayed His might and power by parting the Red Sea; thus, Israel crossed the sea on dry ground.

> **Yahweh raised up Pharaoh in order to declare His Name.**

*And Moses said unto the people, Fear ye not, stand still, and see the salvation (Yahshua) of Yahweh, which he will shew to you to day: (Exodus 14:13a RSB)*

*Raise your staff, stretch out your hand over the sea, and divide the water. Then the Israelites will go through the sea on dry ground. (Exodus 14:16 NOG)*

*And the Israelites went through the middle of the sea on dry ground. The water stood like a wall on their right and on their left. (Exodus 14:22 NOG)*

When Pharaoh and his army chased the children of Israel through the Red Sea, Israel escaped, but Pharaoh and his army were drowned when Yahweh released the waters. After their miraculous deliverance, Moses and the children of Israel invoked the name of Yahweh in songs of praise, acknowledging His power and the power of His right hand, Yahshua.

*Your right hand, O יהוה, has become great in power. Your right hand, O יהוה, has crushed the enemy. (Exodus 15:6 ISR)*

## NEVER FORGET THE NAME OF YAHWEH

In the eighth chapter of Deuteronomy, Israel is instructed repeatedly to never forget Yahweh their Elohim. He specifically uses His personal name and title, not the generic title of LORD and God. Yahweh pleads with His people to never forget His ordinances, including the decree regarding the use of His name, for there is power in His name. Yahweh lays out for Israel the blessings that come with obedience to His instructions.

*Be careful that you don't forget **Yahweh** your **Elohim**. Don't fail to obey his commands, rules, and laws that I'm giving you today. You will eat all you want. You will build nice houses and live in them. Your herds and flocks, silver and gold, and everything else you have will increase. When this happens, be careful that you don't become arrogant and forget **Yahweh** your **Elohim**, who* *brought you out of slavery in Egypt. He was the one who led you through that vast and dangerous desert – a thirsty and arid land, with poisonous snakes and scorpions. He was the one who made water come out of solid rock for you. He was the one who fed you in the desert with manna, which your ancestors had never seen. He did this in order to humble you and test you. But he also did this so that things would go well for you in the end. You may say to yourselves, "I became wealthy because of my own ability and strength." But remember* **Yahweh** *your* **Elohim** *is the one who makes you wealthy. He's confirming the promise which he swore to your ancestors. It's still in effect today. I warn you today that if you forget* **Yahweh** *your* **Elohim** *and follow other gods, and if you serve them and bow down to them, you will certainly be destroyed.* **Yahweh** *is going to destroy other nations as you enter the land. You will be destroyed like them if you don't obey* **Yahweh** *your* **Elohim.** *(Deuteronomy 8:11-20 NOG)*

To paraphrase, Yahweh is bluntly telling Israel, "Listen, I am Yahweh, the Elohim who rescued you from slavery. The other gods of the pagans did not rescue you. I and I alone am your Elohim."

Just as there is power and blessing in proclaiming the name of Yahweh, a curse is pronounced on those who refuse to give glory to His name.

*"If you won't listen and if you won't consider giving honor to my name," says* **Yahweh Tsebaoth** *(Yahweh of Hosts), "then I'll send a*

*curse on you, and I'll curse the blessings you give. Yes, I've already cursed them because you don't carefully consider this." (Malachi 2:2 NOG)*

Wow! In speaking to the priests, Yahweh is warning them that they and the blessings they speak over His people are cursed, if they do not give honor to His name and bless them in His name. The Aaronic blessing of Numbers 6:22-27 immediately comes to mind. The *King James* translation records:

*And the LORD spake unto Moses, saying, Speak unto Aaron and unto his sons, saying, On this wise ye shall bless the children of Israel, saying unto them, The LORD bless thee, and keep thee: The LORD make his face shine upon thee, and be gracious unto thee: The LORD lift up his countenance upon thee, and give thee peace. And they shall put my name upon the children of Israel, and I will bless them.*

The *Names of God* translation records:

**Yahweh** *said to Moses, "Tell Aaron and his sons, 'This is how you will bless the Israelites. Say to them:* **Yahweh** *will bless you and watch over you.* **Yahweh** *will smile on you and be kind to you.* **Yahweh** *will look on you with favor and give you peace.' So whenever they use my name to bless the Israelites, I will bless them." (Numbers 6:22-27 NOG)*

Which of these translations actually honors the name of Yahweh? Yahweh very explicitly states, "Whenever they **use my name** to bless the Israelites, I will bless them." Could it be that some of the blessings spoken over us have not manifested because religious leaders are not using Yahweh's name to bless us, thereby not honoring His name? Could it be the blessings they give "in the name of the LORD" are being turned into curses by Yahweh, because religious leaders refuse to use His name to bless us, even though He specifically instructs them to do so?

The seventeenth chapter of 2 Kings records the evil works of the Israelites, as they worshiped idols and false gods. Herein lies the danger of forsaking Yahweh's name: other gods are embraced right along with Yahweh, with no distinction being made between Yahweh's mighty power and the so-called power of other gods.

*They worshiped **Yahweh** but also served their own gods according to the customs of the nations from which they had come. Today they are still following their customs, as they've done from the beginning. They don't fear **Yahweh** or live by the decrees, customs, teachings, or commands that **Yahweh** gave to the descendants of Jacob (whom he named Israel). When **Yahweh** made a promise to Israel, he commanded, "Never worship other gods, bow down to them, serve them, or sacrifice to them. Instead, worship **Yahweh**, who used his great power and a mighty arm to bring you out of Egypt. Bow down to **Yahweh**, and sacrifice to him. Faithfully obey the laws, rules, teachings, and commands that he wrote for you: 'Never worship other gods. Never forget the promise I made to you. Never worship other gods. Instead, worship **Yahweh** your **Elohim**, and he will* *rescue you from your enemies.'" (2 Kings 17:33-39 NOG)*

When we refuse to glorify the name of Yahweh, we deny His power and the power of His name. We unknowingly lump Him in with all the other gods if we only address Him with the generic title of God. Yahweh is the one true God, and we need to acknowledge His name and recognize the power of His name.

*With your name we can trample those who attack us. (Psalm 44:5b NOG)*

King David recognized the importance and power of Yahweh's name. In 1 Chronicles 29:10-13 (NOG), David rejoiced and sang praises to His name.

*He (David) praised **Yahweh** while the whole assembly watched. David said, "May you be praised, **Yahweh Elohim** of Israel, our father forever and ever. Greatness, power, splendor, glory, and majesty are yours, **Yahweh**, because everything in heaven and on earth is yours. The kingdom is yours, **Yahweh**, and you are honored as head of all things. Riches and honor are in front of you. You rule everything. You hold power and strength in your hands and you can make anyone great and strong. Our **Elohim**, we thank you and praise your wonderful name."*

Nehemiah cried out to God on behalf of the Israelites who had survived Babylonian captivity and for those in Jerusalem. He did not suppress the name of Yahweh when he pleaded with Him to infuse His power to bring relief and deliverance.

*I said, "**Yahweh Elohim** of heaven, great and awe-inspiring **El**, you faithfully keep your promise and show mercy to those who love you and obey your commandments. Open your eyes, and pay close attention with your ears to what I, your servant, am praying. I am praying to you day and night about your servants the Israelites. I confess the sins that we Israelites have committed against you as well as the sins that my father's family and I have committed. We have done you a great wrong. We haven't obeyed the commandments, laws, or regulations that you gave us through your servant Moses. Please remember what you told us through your servant Moses: 'If you are unfaithful, I will scatter you among the nations. But if you return to me and continue to obey my commandments, though your people may be driven to the most distant point on the horizon, **I will come and get you from there and bring you to the place where I chose to put my name**.' (emphasis added) These are your servants and your people whom you have saved by your great power and your strong hand. **Adonay, please pay attention to my prayer and to the prayers of all your other servants who want to worship your name.**" (emphasis added) (Nehemiah 1:5-11a NOG)*

Nehemiah recognized the power of God to restore Israel, in His name, if only Israel would repent, turn back to Him, and obey His instructions once again. I believe Yahweh's instruction regarding the use of His name is one of the ordinances that Israel had forsaken.

Denying God's name does not bring power, but exalting and praising His name does.

*Arise, O **Yahweh**, in your strength. We will sing and make music to praise your power. (Psalm 21:13 NOG)*

When the apostles Peter and John were put on trial by the religious authorities for performing miracles in the name and power of Yahshua, Peter was filled with the Holy Spirit and boldly answered the charges. Note in the following passage of Scripture that Peter makes it clear by what power and in whose name he performed the miracles.

> **Peter was filled with the Holy Spirit.**

*They made Peter and John stand in front of them and then asked, "By what power or in whose name did you do this?" Then Peter, because he was filled with the Holy Spirit, said to them, "Rulers and leaders of the people, today you are cross-examining us about the good we did for a crippled man. You want to know how he was made well. You and all the people of Israel must understand that this man stands in your presence with a healthy body because of the power of **Yeshua** Christ from Nazareth. You crucified **Yeshua** Christ, but God has brought him back to life. He is the stone that the builders rejected, the stone that has become the cornerstone. No one else can save us. Indeed, we can be saved only by the power of the one named **Yeshua** and not by any other person." (Acts 4:7-12 NOG)*

Even though time, as we know it, is drawing to a close, Revelation 19:1 prophesies that Yah <u>will</u> receive the honor and praise due His mighty name!

*And after this I heard a loud voice of a great crowd in the heaven, saying, "Halleluyah! Deliverance and esteem and respect and power to יהוה our Elohim!" (Revelation 19:1 ISR)*

We must recognize the true power in proclaiming the name of Yahweh! In His name, we are set free in every area of our lives. Yahweh is our Shepherd, and He will lead us safely home, blessing us on this journey, as we bring honor and glory to Him and to His mighty name.

*__Yahweh__ is my __Roeh__ (Shepherd). I am never in need. He makes me lie down in green pastures. He leads me beside peaceful waters. He renews my soul. He guides me along paths of righteousness for the sake of His name. (Psalm 23:1-3 NOG)*

## LIVING A DOUBLE STANDARD

Honoring Yahweh's name also means living a life that reflects the highest esteem and respect for our King. We must live a life of holiness and purity.

*"Son of man, when the people of Israel lived in their land, they dishonored it by the way they lived and by everything they did. Their ways were as unclean as a woman's menstrual period... I became concerned about my holy name because my people dishonored it among the nations wherever they went. So tell the people of Israel, 'This is what __Adonay Yahweh__ says: I am about to do something, people of Israel. I will not do this*

*for your sake but for the sake of my holy name, which you have dishonored among the nations wherever you have gone. I will reveal the holiness of my great name, which has been dishonored by the nations, the name that you have dishonored among them. Then the nations will know that I am **Yahweh**, because I will reveal my holiness among you as they watch,'" declares **Adonay Yahweh**. (Ezekiel 36:17, 21-23 NOG)*

*I will make my holy name known among my people Israel, and I will never let them dishonor my holy name again. Then the nations will know that I am **Yahweh**, the Holy One in Israel. (Ezekiel 39:7 NOG)*

Israel dishonored and profaned the name of Yahweh by the lifestyle they embraced. In Ezekiel 36:17 (NOG), Yahweh graphically announces that Israel's *"ways were as unclean as a woman's menstrual period."*

The way to stop dishonoring the name of Yahweh and taking His name in vain is <u>not</u> to stop saying His name. The way we stop taking His name in vain is to repent and live according to His loving instructions. That doesn't mean

**Repent!**

we will live a perfect life, since none of us are perfect, but we need to have a heart that is perfected towards Him and longing to please Him.

*For the eyes of Yahweh run to and fro throughout the whole earth, to shew himself strong in the behalf of them whose heart is perfect toward him. (2 Chronicles 16:9a RSB)*

The word *perfect* in this verse, according to *Strong's Concordance*, number H8003, is *shalem*, which means complete, full, just, made ready, peaceable, quiet. So, Yahweh is looking for someone whose heart is made ready for Him, someone who is seeking to be made complete in Him, someone whose heart is full of Him.

Perfection in this verse does not mean a person who does everything right and never makes a mistake. By the indwelling power of Yahweh's Spirit, though, we will mature spiritually and become a ready witness and testimony to others of Yahweh and the power of His name.

For example, If we proclaim His name and teach His commandment that "Thou shalt not bear false witness," we shouldn't lie and gossip about one another. We cannot exalt Yahweh's name and declare in His name that, "Thou shalt not steal," and then pilfer supplies from our employer. We must live by a higher standard.

*You call yourself a Jew (believer), rely on the laws in Moses' Teachings, brag about your God, know what he wants, and distinguish right from wrong because you have been taught Moses' Teachings. You are confident that you are a guide for the blind, a light to those in the dark, an instructor of ignorant people, and a teacher of children because you have the full content of knowledge and truth in Moses' Teachings. As you teach others, are you failing to teach yourself? As you preach against stealing, are you stealing? As you tell others not to commit adultery, are you committing adultery? As you treat idols with disgust, are you robbing temples? As you brag about the laws in Moses'*

*Teachings, are you dishonoring God by ignoring those laws? As Scripture says, "God's name is cursed among the nations because of you."* (Romans 2:17-24 NOG)

We can't proclaim healing in the name of Yahshua, and then gorge on unhealthy foods and take in substances that pollute and destroy our bodies. We can't speak out against materialism and then treat money as an idol, giving it the power to influence our choices, thereby profaning the very name we claim to exalt. For example, spending every dime of our income on material things and worldly pleasure, while ignoring the plight of the poor disgraces the name of Yahweh and takes His name in vain, brings it to naught, to nothing.

*He has declared to you, O man, what is good. And what does* יהוה *require of you but to do right, and to love kindness, and to walk humbly with your Elohim? (Micah 6:8 ISR)*

Honoring Yahweh involves a rebirth, a new life that reveres the King of the universe. As we exalt Yahweh, we should be convicted to obey Him and truly reflect His image and replicate His kingdom. When we line up with Yahweh's plan and submit to His instructions, we will see real power!

## KING SOLOMON RECOGNIZED THE POWER OF YAHWEH'S NAME

The wisest man in the world, King Solomon, recognized the power of Yahweh's name. Solomon's father, King David, was a man after God's own heart (Acts 13:22 NOG).

*God removed Saul and made David their king. God spoke favorably about David. He said, "I have found that David, son of Jesse, is a man after my own heart. He will do everything I want him to do."*

David instructed his son, Solomon, to cling to Yahweh and follow His commands and instructions; subsequently, Solomon built a temple for Yahweh. Once the temple was completed, Solomon addressed the people.

*When the priests left the holy place, a cloud filled* **Yahweh's** *temple. The priests couldn't serve because of the cloud.* **Yahweh's** *glory filled* **Yahweh's** *temple. Then Solomon said, "***Yahweh** *said he would live in a dark cloud. I certainly have built you a high temple, a home for you to live in permanently." Then the king turned around and blessed the whole assembly of Israel while they were standing. "Thanks be to* **Yahweh Elohim** *of Israel. With his mouth he made a promise to my father David; with his hand he carried it out. He said, 'Ever since I brought my people Israel out of Egypt, I didn't choose any city in any of the tribes of Israel as a place to build a temple for my name. But now I've chosen David to rule my people Israel.' My father David had his heart set on building a temple for the name of* **Yahweh Elohim** *of Israel. However,* **Yahweh** *said to my father David, 'Since you had your heart set on building a temple for my name, your intentions were good. But you must not build the temple. Instead, your own son will build the* temple for my name.' **Yahweh** has kept the promise he made. I have taken my father David's place, and I sit on the throne of Israel as **Yahweh** promised. I've built the temple for the name of **Yahweh Elohim** of Israel. I've made a place there for the ark which contains **Yahweh's** promise that he made to our ancestors when he brought them out of Egypt." (1 Kings 8:10-21 NOG)

We should learn from King Solomon. He stressed several times in the previous passage the importance of building a temple for the name of Yahweh. Solomon recognized the power of Yahweh's name and understood that where Yahweh's name dwelt, His presence and power dwelt, also!

## THE TEMPLE OF YAHWEH TODAY

There are some today who believe that Yahweh's name could only be spoken in His Temple, which was ultimately destroyed in 70 AD. Well, today, the Spirit of Yahweh lives within the followers of Yahshua, and our bodies are now the temple of the living God. Since we are His temple, we are the place that houses the name of Yahweh. We are the temple where the presence and power of Yahweh dwells, today, especially when we acknowledge and exalt His name in His temple.

*Do you not know that your bodies are members of Messiah? Or do you not know that your body is the Dwelling Place of the Set-apart Spirit who is in you, which you have from Elohim, and you are not your own? (1 Corinthians 6:15a,19 ISR)*

*Know ye not that your bodies are the members of Messiah? What? know ye not that your body is the temple of the Holy Spirit which is in you, which ye have of Elohim, and ye are not your own? (1 Corinthians 6:15a,19 RSB)*

*Know ye not that ye are the temple of Yahweh, and that the Spirit of Elohim dwelleth in you? If any man defile the temple of Yahweh, him shall Elohim destroy; for the temple of Yahweh is holy, which temple ye are. (1 Corinthians 3:16-17 RSB)*

*You are that holy temple! (1 Corinthians 3:17b NOG)*

Let me reiterate that Yahweh's name and power dwell in His temple, and His temple is you! You will experience His power and presence as never before when you exalt His name!

# יְהוָה

# Chapter 5
# Value

## HE IS WORTHY

Value is defined as having importance, merit, worth, benefit, significance, profit, usefulness, and meaning. Using this definition, the name of Yahweh has tremendous value. Yahweh is worthy to be praised, loved, adored, and honored.

Yahweh is precious, as is His name. As stated before, we must be ever mindful to speak His name reverently, worshipfully, and respectfully. It takes discipline, temperance, and self-control to refrain from speaking Yahweh's name in vain.

Self-control is a demonstration of the Spirit of God living within the believer. If we are walking in God's Spirit, we will manifest and exhibit the fruit of His Spirit.

*But the fruit of the Spirit is love, joy, peace, patience, kindness, goodness, trustworthiness, gentleness, self-control. Against such there is no Torah. (Galatians 5:22-23 ISR)*

In order to profess the name of Yahweh with reverence and respect, the fruit of Yahweh's Spirit, self-control, must be manifested.

## FREE WILL

Yahweh has given us free will to choose between good and evil, to choose Him or Satan, to choose life or death, blessing or cursing, value or worthlessness.

*Today I offer you life and prosperity or death and destruction. This is what I'm commanding you today: Love **Yahweh** your **Elohim**, follow his directions, and obey his commands, laws, and rules. Then you will live, your population will increase, and **Yahweh** your **Elohim** will bless you in the land that you're about to enter and take possession of. But your hearts might turn away, and you might not listen. You might be tempted to bow down to other gods and worship them. If you do, I tell you today that you will certainly be destroyed. You will not live for a long time in the land that you're going to take possession of when you cross the Jordan River. I call on heaven and earth as witnesses today that I have offered you life or death, blessings or curses. Choose life so that you and your descendants will live. Love **Yahweh** your **Elohim**, obey him, and be loyal to him. (Deuteronomy 30:15-20a NOG)*

Each day we are constantly tested, making countless choices, choosing for God or against Him. To honor, exalt, and bless the name of Yahweh or to blaspheme His name is one of the critical choices we must make. Hiding His name for fear of using it inappropriately is not honorable and has no power, but blessing His name delivers a mighty blow to the adversary! The word

> **We are constantly being tested.**

*bless* means to exalt, extol, laud, sanctify, consecrate, hallow, approve, endorse, and commend. Notice how the following Scripture verses demonstrate how we, as believers, should bless the name of Yahweh our God.

*O **Yahweh**, our **Adonay**, how majestic is your name throughout the earth! Your glory is sung above the heavens. (Psalm 8:1 NOG)*

*O sing unto Yahweh a new song: sing unto Yahweh, all the earth. Sing unto Yahweh, bless his name; shew forth his salvation from day to day. (Psalm 96:1-2 RSB)*

*Enter into his gates with thanksgiving, and into his courts with praise: be thankful unto him, and bless his name. (Psalm 100:4 RSB)*

*Bless Yahweh, O my soul: and all that is within me, bless his holy name. (Psalm 103:1 RSB)*

*Hallelujah! You servants of **Yahweh**, praise him. Praise the name of **Yahweh**. Thank the name of **Yahweh** now and forever. From where the sun rises to where the sun sets, the name of **Yahweh** should be praised. (Psalm 113:1-3 NOG)*

*And (Job) said, Naked came I out of my mother's womb, and naked shall I return thither: Yahweh gave, and Yahweh hath taken away; blessed be the name of Yahweh. (Job 1:21 RSB)*

To bless the name of Yahweh means to exalt His name above everyone and above everything. I choose to bless His name, not just His title. I choose to bless the name of Yahweh. HalleluYah!

## A GREATER BOND

As I stated earlier, there is nothing wrong with calling Yahweh God, for He is God. There is nothing wrong with calling Yahweh LORD, for He is LORD. Nevertheless, speaking His name adds another layer of value, worth, and power, and elicits a richer, deeper experience of intimacy. Knowing the name of the One we love and speaking His name in worship draws us nearer to His throne, nearer to Him.

Knowing the personal name of Yahweh enriches my relationship with Him, and it creates a greater bond between us. Knowing His name and the power it brings makes me fall deeper and deeper in love with Him. When I proclaim, "Yahweh," and worshipfully, lovingly utter His name, I am suddenly elevated above my circumstances. Singing praises to Yahweh is an experience like no other! Declaring, "Yahweh," is like taking in a breath and exhaling it. Speaking His name is like breathing Him in. The very act of saying, "Yahweh," reminds me that I cannot breathe in if He does not breathe out. I cannot live if He does not give me the breath of life.

*And Yahweh Elohim formed man of the dust of the ground, and breathed into his nostrils the breath of life; and man became a living soul. (Genesis 2:7 RSB)*

It is extremely important to value and treasure Almighty Yahweh and distinguish Him from other mighty ones, gods, and idols. Yahweh is great and greatly to be praised!

*For great is Yahweh, and greatly to be praised: he also is to be feared above all mighty ones. For all the mighty ones of the people are idols: but Yahweh made the heavens. (1 Chronicles 16:25-26 RSB)*

We must stop hiding His name and begin to bless His holy name! We cannot ignore His instruction regarding His name any longer. It has as much value as His other instructions.

*This command I'm giving you today isn't too hard for you or beyond your reach. It's not in heaven. You don't have to ask, "Who will go to heaven to get this command for us so that we can hear it and obey it?" This command isn't on the other side of the sea. You don't have to ask, "Who will cross the sea to get it for us so that we can hear it and obey it?" No, these words are very near you. They're in your mouth and in your heart so that you will obey them. (Deuteronomy 30:11-14 NOG)*

Yahshua has brought the name of Yahweh near to us. He came all the way from heaven so that we may hear His instruction on many things, including His name and the name of His Father.

## A HIDDEN JEWEL

Yahweh's name is a hidden jewel buried in plain sight in Scripture over 6,800 times, disguised as the word LORD. Unlike the title LORD, however, the name of Yahweh is rich in meaning. The word *rich* is defined as fertile, fruitful, productive, lush, full, abundant, wealthy, prosperous, intense, splendid, valuable, magnificent, strong, powerful, and vibrant. These are all words that describe Yahweh!

*And I will give thee the treasures of darkness, and hidden riches of secret places, that thou mayest know that I, Yahweh, which call thee by thy name, am the Elohim of Israel. (Isaiah 45:3 RSB)*

In Exodus 33:19a (NOG), in response to Moses' request to see Yahweh's glory, Yahweh tells Moses:

**Yahweh** *said, "I will let all my goodness pass in front of you, and there I will call out my name 'Yahweh.'"*

Experiencing Yahweh's vibrancy and perceiving the richness of His glory is achieved, in part, by knowing His name. *Strong's Concordance* defines *know* (H3045, yada) as recognize, discern, acknowledge, comprehend, respect, and understand, just to name a few. So, knowing Yahweh's name is acknowledging and recognizing Him as the One true living God, and confessing Him as the Eternal Self-Existent God, the One who is the Creator and Sustainer of all things.

If Yahweh had not wanted His name to be known, He would not have included it in Scripture almost 7,000 times. Even though well-meaning, well-intentioned people have replaced Yahweh's name with LORD, that does not nullify His decree regarding His name and give us a license to obliterate His name from Scripture and from our vocabulary. We cannot erase the name of the One that we claim to love.

If Yahshua should tarry and not come soon, I believe His name will also be erased and/or disguised. Actually, that attempt has already been made by the enemy, because not many people know that our Savior's name was originally spoken in the first century as Yahshua. The name that will be next on the adversary's hit list will be Jesus. There are people in today's culture who take the name of Jesus in vain without batting an eye and use His name as a curse word. Well-meaning people may build a

**Jesus' name has become a curse word.**

fence around the name of Jesus and ban its use, just like well-meaning people wanted to protect the name of Yahweh by forbidding people to speak His name. I see the same fate for the name of the Messiah if we do not comprehend the true power available to us by appropriately speaking the name of God.

Yahweh gave us free will so that we could choose between life and death, good and evil. Sin will not be eradicated by reducing the choices. We can choose to speak Yahweh's name or suppress it. Each of us has a personal responsibility to choose blessing or cursing for ourselves. No one should have the power to make the choice for us by hiding His name or forbidding it to be spoken. He gave us His Name for a reason. Could it be so we can proclaim it?

## YAHWEH IN THE NEW TESTAMENT

Because modern translations of the New Testament were derived from Greek, Yahweh's name has been obliterated from the New Testament. The Greek word for god is theos, and it can refer to countless gods. At the time of Yahshua's earthly ministry, theos could refer to the one true God, Yahweh, or it could refer to Zeus, Apollo, Hermes, Poseidon, or any number of Greek gods. The Greek word for lord is kurios, and it's been watered down to merely mean "sir" by those who deny that Yahshua is God.

Unlike the Tanakh (referred to as the Old Testament), which used specific Hebrew words to describe Yahweh and His specific attributes, such as Yahweh Rapha (Healer), Yahweh Rohe (Shepherd), Yahweh Nissi (Banner), Yahweh Yireh (Provider), Yahweh Tsidkenu (Righteousness), etc., the Greek words describing Yahweh and Yahshua are simply Theos for God and Kurios for Lord, and Lord is not even written in all capital letters as in the Old Testament.

Even though there are clear references to Scriptures in the Tanakh where the name Yahweh should have been written in the New Testament, the Greek translation merely refers to God or Lord. Yahshua quotes Isaiah 61:1 in Luke 4:18-19. Following is the *King James* translation and a translation from the *Restoration Study Bible*.

*The Spirit of the Lord is upon me, because he hath anointed me to preach the gospel to the poor; he hath sent me to heal the brokenhearted, to preach deliverance to the captives, and recovering of sight to the blind, to set at liberty them that are bruised, to preach the acceptable year of the Lord. (Luke 4:18-19 KJV)*

*The Spirit of my Sovereign Yahweh is upon me; because Yahweh hath anointed me to preach good tidings unto the meek; he hath sent me to bind up the brokenhearted, to proclaim liberty to the captives, and the opening of the prison to them that are bound; to proclaim the acceptable year of Yahweh ... (Isaiah 61:1-2a RSB)*

You can clearly see that the Scripture Yahshua quoted from the Old Testament specifies Yahweh, but the Greek New Testament uses the general title Lord. Did Yahshua speak the name of His Father, Yahweh, or did He only speak His title, LORD?

I believe part of the reason the religious leaders wanted to get rid of Yahshua was because He would not suppress the name of Yahweh. In addition, Yahshua clearly, on numerous occasions, referred to Yahweh as His Father, which also exasperated the religious to no end.

## YAH STILL HAS VALUE

Even though the name Yahweh has been replaced in the Old Testament thousands of times, there are still traces of His name that have survived censorship. Since Hebrew names describe the person assigned that name, the name of Yah is still somewhat evident in some of the names in the Old Testament.

For example, Jeremiah in Hebrew is Yirme**yah**u, which means "Yahweh has uplifted." The name Isaiah or Yesha'**yah**u means "Yahweh has saved." Nehemiah or Nechem**yah** means "Comforted by Yahweh." You can see that within Jeremiah, Isaiah, and Nehemiah is the name of Yah. The "iah" of their names is pronounced Yah, which stands for Yahweh. Each of these names proclaim the value of Yahweh in their lives, which means their parents understood the value of His name. Even though Yah's name may be hidden today, His name lives on in His prophets, because every time we say Jeremiah, Isaiah, or Nehemiah, we speak the name of Yah, even though the spelling "iah" masks His name. Other names with Yah in them are Obadiah (Ovad**yah**), meaning servant of Yahweh; Zephaniah (Tzefan**yah**), meaning Yahweh has hidden; Zechariah (Zekhar**yah**), meaning Yahweh remembers; and Benaiah (Bena**yah**), meaning Yahweh has built up.

> **The name of Yah lives on in His prophets.**

These are just a few biblical names that contain the name of Yah. There are even names today that have the name Yah within them. One prominent person with Yah in his name is Benjamin Netan**yah**u, Prime Minister of Israel (as of this writing). The name Netanyahu means "Yahweh has given."

Another biblical expression containing the name of Yah that retains its value today is the word hallelujah, which is actually spelled halleluYah. The "jah" in the English transliteration of hallelujah is actually pronounced Yah. Hallelujah means, "Praise you, Yah."

For those who feel we don't know how to pronounce the name of Yahweh, and therefore shouldn't speak His name, it is absolutely certain that the first three letters are pronounced Yah, and biblical scholars have determined that the last three letters, "weh," are pronounced as "way."

## GIVE HONOR WHERE HONOR IS DUE

We <u>must</u> give Yahweh the honor due Him and the honor due His name. We should never disrespect the Creator of all things by refusing to address Him by name. We need to respect the name of Yah, whether addressing Yahweh or Yahshua.

Many today think Yahshua was just a good man, a good teacher, or maybe even a prophet. Yahshua, however, is God Almighty, Yahweh in the flesh, who walked among us, and who gave His life for us, as the Lamb of Yah, so that we could live eternally with Him.

We must give Him the respect He truly deserves. When we speak the name Yahshua, we acknowledge He has saved us by the power of Yahweh. He came to earth as the living Word and demonstrated how we should live. Yahshua gave the supreme sacrifice and freed us forever from the clutches of death, hell, and the grave.

When we say Yahweh, we acknowledge that He is eternal and sovereign, with no beginning and no end, and that He relies on absolutely no one nor nothing to sustain Him or keep Him going. We recognize He alone holds all things in order and is our beginning and end, the first and the last.

He is supreme, and there is none above Him! Yes, a name is very important. Satan, of course, wants to devalue the name of Yahweh by blotting it out of our memory, but we must not let His name be obliterated. We must reverently profess the name Yahweh, who is God Almighty, El Shaddai, the mightiest of all!

יהוה
צֶבָא

# Chapter 6
# Legacy

## BEST KEPT SECRET

I would venture to say that Yahweh's name is probably one of the best kept secrets in the world today. A secret is designed to keep something or someone from being seen or known.

*Who hath ascended up into heaven, or descended? who hath gathered the wind in his fists? who hath bound the waters in a garment? who hath established all the ends of the earth? what is his name, and what is his son's name, if thou canst tell? (Proverbs 30:4 RSB)*

Since Yahshua came in His Father's name, Yahweh, I doubt that He would want to keep the name of His Father the world's greatest secret.

*I am come in my Father's name, and ye receive me not: if another shall come in his own name, him ye will receive. (John 5:43 RSB)*

*"I won't be in the world much longer, but they are in the world, and I'm coming back to you. Holy Father, keep them safe by the power of your name, the name that you gave me, so that their unity may be like ours. While I was with them, I kept them safe by the power of your name, the name that you gave me." (John 17:11-12a NOG)*

*"I have made your name known to them, and I will make it known so that the love you have for me will be in them and I will be in them." (John 17:26 NOG)*

If Yahweh wanted to keep His name a secret, He certainly wouldn't have revealed it thousands of times in Scripture. While we live in these mortal bodies, sin keeps us from doing what is right, and Yahweh has always known that. So, why would He entrust humanity with such a huge secret? The eternally self-existent God, Yahweh, always had a plan to keep His name alive forever!

*Again **Elohim** said to Moses, "This is what you must say to the people of Israel: **Yahweh Elohim** of your ancestors, the **Elohim** of Abraham, Isaac, and Jacob, has sent me to you. This is my name forever. This is my title throughout every generation." (Exodus 3:15 NOG)*

*In this house, and in Jerusalem, which I have chosen out of all tribes of Israel, will I put my name for ever: (2 Kings 21:7b RSB)*

*In Elohim we boast all the day long, and praise thy name for ever. Selah. (Psalm 44:8 RSB)*

*So will I sing praise unto thy name for ever, that I may daily perform my vows. (Psalm 61:8 RSB)*

*I will praise thee, O Yahweh my Elohim, with all my heart: and I will glorify thy name for evermore. (Psalm 86:12 RSB)*

*My mouth shall speak the praise of Yahweh: and let all flesh bless his holy name for ever and ever. (Psalm 145:21 RSB)*

## WHAT IS A LEGACY?

A legacy is defined as an inheritance, heritage, endowment, gift, settlement, birthright, or anything handed down from the past. From the foundation of the world, Yahweh created a legacy for those who would believe in and follow Him.

When Yahweh gave His commandments through Moses, He already knew that humanity would sin and fail to observe His laws; therefore, He made an atonement for sin through His Son, Yahshua, whereby we are pardoned and forgiven of our sin. Israel's offerings of grain, cattle, and fowl could not cleanse them from sin. It is only the blood of Yahshua, the guiltless, spotless Lamb of Yah, that cleanses us from all unrighteousness.

*But if we walk in the light, as he is in the light, we have fellowship one with another, and the blood of Yahshua Messiah his Son cleanseth us from all sin. If we say that we have no sin, we deceive ourselves, and the truth is not in us. If we confess our sins, he is faithful and just to forgive us our sins, and to cleanse us from all unrighteousness. (1 John 1:7-9 RSB)*

This is indeed a legacy that is everlasting and will not be stolen from the people of Yah, who proclaim His name and have chosen not to suppress it nor change it.

*Terror and dread will fall on them. Because of the power of your arm (Yahshua), they will be petrified until your people pass by, O **Yahweh**, until the people you purchased pass by. You will bring them and plant them on your own mountain, the place where you live, O **Yahweh**, the holy place that you built with your own hands, O **Adonay**. Yahweh will rule as king forever and ever. (Exodus 15:16-18 NOG)*

*Then they that feared Yahweh spake often one to another: and Yahweh hearkened, and heard it, and a book of remembrance was written before him for them that feared Yahweh, and that thought upon his name. (Malachi 3:16 RSB)*

## THE FATHER AND SON ARE ONE

The Shema is the central prayer in the Jewish prayer book (Siddur) and is often the first section of Scripture that a Jewish child learns. The Shema is an affirmation of Judaism and a declaration of faith in one God.

*Hear, O Yisrael: יהוה our Elohim, יהוה is one! (Deuteronomy 6:4 ISR)*

When one of the scribes came to Yahshua and asked Him which was the greatest commandment, Yahshua answered:

*And יהושע (Yahshua) answered him, "The first of all the commands is, 'Hear, O Yisrael, יהוה (Yahweh) our Elohim, יהוה is one.'" (Mark 12:29 ISR)*

We serve one God, one LORD, one Master, who is Yah. Zechariah declares a day is coming when Yahweh will be the only name of the King. HalleluYah!

*And יהוה shall be Sovereign over all the earth. In that day there shall be one יהוה and His Name one. (Zechariah 14:9 ISR)*

Acknowledging the holy name of Yahweh gives recognition to and proclaims the eternally self-existent God of the Old Testament; acknowledging the name of Yahshua recognizes and proclaims Yahweh in Yahshua, who came to sacrifice His own life to redeem us, deliver us, save us from death, hell, and the grave.

*But to us there is but one Elohim, the Father, of whom are all things, and we in him; and one Master Yahshua Messiah, by whom are all things, and we by him. (1 Corinthians 8:6 RSB)*

There are several references in Scripture that speak of God in Christ. Christ is the Greek word for Messiah. It is important to know to whom we are referring. It is Yahweh in Christ (Messiah).

*I press toward the mark for the prize of the high calling of Yahweh in Messiah Yahshua. (Philippians 3:14 RSB)*

*In every thing give thanks: for this is the will of Yahweh in Messiah Yahshua concerning you. (1 Thessalonians 5:18 RSB)*

Our legacy and inheritance from Yahweh is guaranteed through the atonement of Yahshua the Messiah. Included in the Apostle Paul's letter to the Ephesians is a clear reference to the oneness of Elohim (God).

*There is one body, and one Spirit, even as ye are called in one hope of your calling; One Master, one faith, one baptism, One El (God) and Father of all, who is above all, and through all, and in you all. But unto every one of us is given grace according to the measure of the gift of Messiah. Wherefore he saith, WHEN HE ASCENDED UP ON HIGH, HE LED CAPTIVITY CAPTIVE, AND GAVE GIFTS UNTO MEN. (Now that he ascended, what is it but that he also descended first into the lower parts of the earth? He that descended is the same also that ascended up far above all heavens, that he might fill all things.) (Ephesians 4:4-10 RSB)*

Verse 10 of Ephesians 4 refers back to Proverbs 30:4.

*Who hath ascended up into heaven, or descended? who hath gathered the wind in his fists? who hath bound the waters in a garment? who hath established all the ends of the earth? what is his name, and what is his son's name, if thou canst tell? (Proverbs 30:4 RSB)*

Yahweh blessed us with a legacy in time past that would ensure a treasure that no man could ever give.

*Favour to you and peace from Elohim our Father and the Master יהושע (Yahshua) Messiah ... who is the pledge of our inheritance, until the redemption of the purchased possession, to the praise of His esteem. (Ephesians 1:2,14 ISR)*

*...looking for the blessed expectation and esteemed appearance of the great Elohim and our Saviour יהושע (Yahshua) Messiah, who gave Himself for us, to redeem us from all lawlessness and to cleanse for Himself a people, His own possession, ardent for good works. (Titus 2:13-14 ISR)*

## ALL SCRIPTURE IS GOD-BREATHED

Scripture is vitally important, if believers are going to grow in their walk with Yah.

*All scripture is given by inspiration of Yahweh, and is profitable for doctrine, for reproof, for correction, for instruction in righteousness: That the man of Elohim may be perfect, throughly furnished unto all good works. (2 Timothy 3:16-17 RSB)*

The Word of Yah is powerful, helping the believer to discern good and evil, right and wrong.

*For the word of Elohim is quick and powerful, and sharper than any twoedged sword, piercing even to the dividing asunder of soul and spirit, and of the joints and marrow, and is a discerner of the thoughts and intents of the heart. (Hebrews 4:12 RSB)*

Only the Word of Yah can help us discern the truth. Is it really the intention of Yahweh to keep His name a secret, when He revealed it more than 6,800 times in His own Word?

*How long will these prophets continue to lie and deceive? They tell each other the dreams they had, because they want to make my people forget my name, as their ancestors forgot my name because of Baal. (Jeremiah 23:26-27 NOG)*

*Behold, the days come, saith Yahweh, that I will raise unto David a righteous Branch, and a King shall reign and prosper, and shall execute judgment and justice in the earth. In his days Judah shall be saved, and Israel shall dwell safely: and this is his name whereby he shall be called, YAHWEH OUR RIGHTEOUSNESS. (Jeremiah 23:5-6 RSB)*

Jeremiah 23:5-6 is astonishing in that it prophesies the coming of the Messiah, who will be called Yahweh. Even though verse 5 clearly refers to Yahshua, verse 6 says His name will be Yahweh. This shows again the oneness of Yah. He is not three separate Gods. He is one Elohim. As mentioned before, the term El is the singular form of the Hebrew term for God, and Elohim is the plural form. Yahweh is referred to as Elohim, because He has many attributes. For instance, He is Yahweh Melech (King), Yahweh Maon (Dwelling Place), Yahweh Machseh (Refuge), Yahweh Magen (Shield) etc. Even though He has many attributes and many titles, His

> **Yahweh has many attributes.**

personal name still remains Yahweh. He is one God, not many gods. Yahweh longs to make His name known again.

*"Father, give glory to your name." A voice from heaven said, "I have given it glory, and I will give it glory again." (John 12:28 NOG)*

There is coming a day when Yahweh will give His renewed name to His people. Be assured that the name of Yah will not be lost forever. In His Revelation to the Apostle John on the island of Patmos, Yahshua proclaimed:

*"He who has an ear, let him hear what the Spirit says to the assemblies. To him who overcomes I shall give some of the hidden manna to eat. And I shall give him a white stone, and on the stone a renewed Name written which no one knows except him who receives it." (Revelation 2:17 ISR)*

*I know thy works: behold, I have set before thee an open door, and no man can shut it: for thou hast a little strength, and hast kept my word, and hast not denied my name. (Revelation 3:8 RSB)*

*He who overcomes, I shall make him a supporting post in the Dwelling Place of My Elohim, and he shall by no means go out. And I shall write on him the Name of My Elohim and the name of the city of My Elohim, the renewed Yerushalayim, which comes down out of the heaven from My Elohim, and My renewed Name. (Revelation 3:12 ISR)*

*I looked, and the lamb was standing on Mount Zion. There were 144,000 people with him who had his name and his Father's name written on their foreheads. (Revelation 14:1 NOG)*

*And I saw like a sea of glass mixed with fire, and those overcoming the beast and his image and his mark and the number of his name, standing on the sea of glass, holding harps of Elohim. And they sing the song of Mosheh (Moses) the servant of Elohim, and the song of the Lamb, saying, "Great and marvellous are Your works, יהוה El Shaddai! Righteous and true are Your ways, O Sovereign of the set-apart ones! Who shall not fear You, O יהוה, and esteem Your Name? Because You alone are kind. Because all nations shall come and worship before You, for Your righteousnesses have been made manifest." (Revelation 15:2-4 ISR)*

*There will no longer be any curse. The throne of God and the lamb will be in the city. His servants will worship him and see his face. His name will be on their foreheads. (Revelation 22:3-4 NOG)*

Notice in the preceding verse there is one throne, one God, who is the Lamb, and one name on the forehead of His servants. Yahweh cut away a piece of Himself to redeem mankind. He cut a covenant not with mankind, because that covenant had failed long ago. Yahweh's covenant is with His Son, ratified by blood. It was not a new covenant; it was a renewed covenant that would bring salvation from sin, death, and hell, and rescue all who would believe in

> **Yahweh's covenant is with His Son.**

118

Yahweh's only begotten Son, Yahshua, as prophesied by David in the second chapter of the Psalms.

*I will announce **Yahweh's** decree. He said to me: "You are my Son. Today I have become your Father. Ask me, and I will give you the nations as your inheritance and the ends of the earth as your own possession." (Psalm 2:7-8 NOG)*

How extraordinarily beautiful to know that we not only <u>have</u> an inheritance from Yahweh; we <u>are</u> an inheritance, a gift from Father to Son. Yahshua is shepherding us through this journey, leading us home to our ultimate destination: eternal paradise with Yahweh.

This is our incredible legacy, that Yahweh's name will not be lost and that we will live with Him, in His name, for all eternity. There is no inheritance as wonderful as this. We have eternal life in Him in more ways than we could ever imagine! This is just one small revelation given by Yahweh of our legacy. There is so much more that He has not yet revealed; but as we seek Him with our whole heart, He will reveal more and more.

*And you shall seek Me, and shall find Me, when you search for Me with all your heart. (Jeremiah 29:13 ISR)*

The legacy of Yahweh to us, through Yahushua, is that we will be one with Him by the sovereign authority and power of His name!

יהוה
יֵשַׁע

# Chapter 7
# Salvation

## HIS NAME IS WONDERFUL

The name of our God is more magnificent and wonderful than mere words could ever express. The prophet Isaiah gives an amazing description of our all-powerful, eternal King and describes Him in extraordinarily beautiful and very intriguing language. Isaiah starts by unveiling a mighty Deliverer, whom he declares will come forth through the birth of a child, a Son. Just a few words later, Isaiah discloses that from this humble birth comes The Mighty God and The Everlasting Father!

*For unto us a child is born, unto us a son is given: and the government shall be upon his shoulder: and his name shall be called Wonderful, Counsellor, The mighty El (God), The everlasting Father, The Prince of Peace. (Isaiah 9:6 RSB)*

What a remarkable description of the One who was, who is, and who is to come! Our King is coming soon. He will not fail us, and He will never, ever leave us nor forsake us.

No more will the adversary rob us of our rightful inheritance. Our King will reign forever and of His kingdom there will be no end. Our Savior and Redeemer will rule for all eternity.

Although there are many languages in the world, we can be grateful that we can now know the name of Yahweh and proclaim it with conviction. Whether you speak English, Hebrew, Spanish, Japanese, or another language, the name of Yahweh still remains a strong tower, and the righteous run into it and are safe! We can be thankful that our God is mighty to save, by the power of His name.

*The stone which the builders rejected has become the chief corner-stone. This was from יהוה, it is marvellous in our eyes. This is the day יהוה has made, let us rejoice and be glad in it. I pray, O יהוה, please save; I pray, O יהוה, please send prosperity. Blessed is He who is coming in the Name of יהוה! We shall bless you from the house of Yahweh. (Psalm 118:22-26 ISR)*

In Matthew 23:37-39 (ISR), Yahshua makes a staggering prophetic statement that links beautifully to the preceding scripture verse, Psalm 118:26, and gives Israel a stunning clue to when He will return.

*"Yerushalayim, Yerushalayim, killing the prophets and stoning those who are sent to her! How often I wished to gather your children together, the way a hen gathers her chickens*

*under her wings, but you would not! See! Your house is left to you laid waste, for I say to you, from now on you shall by no means see Me, until you say, 'Blessed is He who is coming in the Name of* יהוה *(Yahweh)!'"*

Yahshua is coming back not just when Israel calls Him Lord, but when they confess that Yahshua is Yahweh! Two things happen here. Israel receives Yahshua as Messiah and King, and they confess His name. Today, most of Israel and some Gentiles, who have bought the lie, refuse to speak the name Yahweh; but in the end, they will.

**Yahweh** *is my strength and my fortress, my refuge in times of trouble. Nations come to you from the most distant parts of the world and say, "Our ancestors have inherited lies, worthless and unprofitable gods." "People can't make gods for themselves. They aren't really gods. That is what I will teach them. This time I will make my power and my strength known to them. Then they will know that my name is* **Yahweh.**" *(Jeremiah 16:19-21 NOG)*

Yahshua will return when Israel finally speaks His name and recognizes Him. Yahweh's name has been covered up and kept a secret, but the secret is out! His name is now known by a remnant and being taught to a whole new generation of believers, both Jew and Gentile. No matter how much the enemy has tried to hide, blot out, and obliterate the name of our God, His name lives on!

## The secret is out!

*Neither is there salvation in any other: for there is none other name under heaven given among men, whereby we must be saved. (Acts 4:12 RSB)*

*For I am not ashamed of the good news of Messiah: for it is the power of Elohim unto salvation to every one that believeth; to the Jew first, and also to the Greek. (Romans 1:16 RSB)*

*I write to you, little children, because your sins have been forgiven on account of His Name. (1 John 2:12 ISR)*

*Even so, come, Master Yahshua. (Revelation 22:20b RSB)*

*The grace of our Sovereign Yahshua the Messiah be with you all. Amen. (Revelation 22:21 RSB)*

The last word in Scripture is "Amen," translated as, "So be it!" So be it, Yahshua! Salvation come!

# יהוה

# Conclusion

I hope and pray that you have received valuable information that will help you in your walk with Yah. The names Yahweh and Yahshua are powerful and are to be proclaimed and exalted now and throughout all eternity! The anthem and song we raise to our King should be an exaltation of praise and thanksgiving for the wonderful things He has done, continues to do, and will forever do for His people. We can live an abundant life filled with blessed hope and expectation in Yah! Yahweh's declaration is:

*I know the plans that I have for you, declares* **Yahweh.** *They are plans for peace and not disaster, plans to give you a future filled with hope. (Jeremiah 29:11 NOG)*

And our response to Yahweh must be:

*I will give thanks to you forever for what you have done. In the presence of your godly people, I will wait with hope **in your good name** (emphasis added). (Psalm 52:9 NOG)*

I pray that you are blessed by the message Yahweh has given me to share with you. I also pray that you have accepted Yahshua as Savior and Master of your life and recognize Him as Almighty Yahweh! All you have to do is say, "Yes, Yahshua, I receive you as my Savior and Master. I believe that you are the Almighty God, Yahweh, who came in the flesh and died for my sin, whereby I am forgiven. I will live <u>for</u> you and <u>with</u> you for the rest of my days and throughout eternity!"

Yahshua is the door to eternal life, and if Yahshua is your Master, the following blessing belongs to you.

By the power and authority of Abba Yahweh, and in the name of Yahshua, I declare and decree upon you Yahweh's Word from Numbers 6:24-26. As His child, you can be assured and confident that, in Yahshua:

Yahweh will bless you and keep you, present you with gifts, and guard you with a hedge of protection.

Yahweh will make His face shine upon you, be gracious to you, illuminate the wholeness of His being toward you, and bring order to your life.

Yahweh will provide you with love, sustenance, and friendship.

Yahweh will lift up His countenance upon you and give you peace.

Yahweh will lift up the wholeness of His being toward you and set in place everything you need.

Yahweh will give you His shalom (peace), so that you will be whole and complete, nothing missing, nothing lacking, and nothing broken.

I pray that you will continue to draw even nearer to Yahweh as you continue to contemplate:

## "What's in a name?"

www.ingramcontent.com/pod-product-compliance
Lightning Source LLC
Chambersburg PA
CBHW061741020426
42331CB00006B/1314